T5-CQA-333

allyssa BeAnne

PRAISE FOR *LOVE THAT LASTS*

"Being single, this book encouraged me greatly and helped me realize how loved I am by God. Jeff and Alyssa are so personal, which allowed me to relate to their experiences and hold tight to what God says about my own sexuality."

    —Sarah, college student, single

"We are starting our fortieth year of marriage and wholeheartedly can recommend this book to married couples, young and old."

    —Bob and Dani, married thirty-nine years

"As someone whose marriage did not last, this was the most encouraging relationship book I've ever read. Jeff and Alyssa share insightful reflections and powerful truths they learned as they unpacked the baggage they brought with them into marriage. No matter your upbringing, spiritual journey, or relationship status, *Love That Lasts* has something for everyone."

    —Leslie, middle school teacher, single

"We wish we had this book when we were newly married! It's so refreshing to read a relationship book from a couple who is in the thick of it. *Love That Lasts* is full of transparency and truth. Jeff and Alyssa are navigating marriage with love and grace and growth and will encourage you to do the same."

    —Nate and Jenna, married ten years

"From beginning to end, this book offers encouragement and insight into relationships in a refreshing and easy to understand way. We believe there is something for everyone in this book!"

    —Tyler and Bailey, dating for four years

"Our own journey included an amazing first year of marriage filled with excitement that was quickly overshadowed by multiple negative pregnancy tests. After two failed IVF cycles, while in medical residency working eighty-plus hours, we are finally finishing this chapter of our lives. *Love That Lasts* is like a map guiding us through those times, shedding light on so much darkness, and pointing us toward a brighter future and oneness."

    —Kevin and Lauren, married four years and soon to be parents!

"It is so refreshing and encouraging to read Jeff and Alyssa's story. They are real and honest, and through their vulnerability I found healing—healing from my fears and from my doubts that there can be such a thing as a God-centered, healthy marriage. Everyone, no matter what stage of a relationship they're in (or even if they're single like me), needs to read this story of healing, redemption, and love that lasts."

—Cara, college student, single

"The Bethke's combine honest storytelling and teaching so skillfully, allowing readers to instantly relate. You will walk away inspired and encouraged to find lasting love in your own life."

—Jeff, young professional, single, ready to mingle

"Regardless of our experiences we have baggage to unpack and wounds to heal, but we were made for so much more than something temporary, we were made for a love that lasts."

—Rebekah Harmon, married three years, age forty-two

"Jeff and Alyssa invite us into the detail of their lives with total humility and generosity! The telling of their individual pasts and marriage story is configured with fundamental biblical truth that illuminates God's design for romantic relationships. This book uncovers brokenness as our reality but redirects us toward freedom and renewal in Christ—an encouraging read for young people (and old!)."

—Keri Scholte, UCLA college student

"This book offers important insight into God's plan for our relationships. In Ephesians 2:10, Paul reminds us that we are God's handiwork, created to do good works which He has prepared for us to do. *Love That Lasts* reminds us that our relationships are an important part of that larger plan."

—Alek Ball, master's student

"A wonderful and personal look at marriage for those who are starting the journey. Our takeaway from the book, and thirty-nine years of marriage, is to realize that if you think marriage is what you make it, you are wrong. A marriage governed by the love of Jesus is what makes you into a strong and emotionally happy couple. And it becomes the biggest blessing possible this side of heaven. Read and believe."

—Jay and Patti Salevan, married thirty-nine years

"I can't believe how much I related to Jeff and Alyssa as I read through their love story. *Love That Lasts* demonstrates grace in dating and in marriage. My teenage children will certainly benefit from reading about the trials they faced in college and dating."

—Paige, married twenty-three years

LOVE THAT LASTS

LOVE THAT LASTS

HOW WE DISCOVERED GOD'S BETTER WAY FOR LOVE, DATING, MARRIAGE, AND SEX

JEFFERSON AND ALYSSA BETHKE

NELSON BOOKS

An Imprint of Thomas Nelson

© 2017 by Jefferson Bethke and Alyssa Bethke

All rights reserved. No portion of this book may be reproduced, stored in a retrieval system, or transmitted in any form or by any means—electronic, mechanical, photocopy, recording, scanning, or other—except for brief quotations in critical reviews or articles, without the prior written permission of the publisher.

Published in Nashville, Tennessee, by Nelson Books, an imprint of Thomas Nelson. Nelson Books and Thomas Nelson are registered trademarks of HarperCollins Christian Publishing, Inc.

Published in association with Yates & Yates, www.yates2.com.

Thomas Nelson titles may be purchased in bulk for educational, business, fund-raising, or sales promotional use. For information, please e-mail SpecialMarkets@ThomasNelson.com.

Any Internet addresses, phone numbers, or company or product information printed in this book are offered as a resource and are not intended in any way to be or to imply an endorsement by Thomas Nelson, nor does Thomas Nelson vouch for the existence, content, or services of these sites, phone numbers, companies, or products beyond the life of this book.

Unless otherwise noted, Scripture quotations are taken from the ESV® Bible (The Holy Bible, English Standard Version®), copyright © 2001 by Crossway, a publishing ministry of Good News Publishers. Used by permission. All rights reserved.

Scripture quotations marked NASB are taken from New American Standard Bible®, Copyright © 1960, 1962, 1963, 1968, 1971, 1972, 1973, 1975, 1977, 1995 by The Lockman Foundation. Used by permission. (www.Lockman.org)

ISBN 978–0-7180-3919-6 (eBook)
ISBN 978–0-7180-3918-9 (TP)
ISBN 978-1-4002-0820-3 (signed)

Library of Congress Control Number: 2017937058

Printed in the United States of America

17 18 19 20 21 LSC 10 9 8 7 6 5 4 3 2 1

To Kinsley & Kannon—

While our love is imperfect,

We hope, through our picture, you come to know

The One who is.

Love, Mom and Dad

CONTENTS

CONTENTS

A NOTE TO OUR READERS

Alyssa and I received a message from a woman on Facebook the other day. She shared with us that her friends—a husband and wife—had recently completed our 31 Day Challenge series. They had been on the brink of divorce and, as a last-ditch effort, decided to read our devotionals, *31 Days to Love & Encourage Him* and the complementary book *31 Days to Love & Encourage Her*. By an act of God's grace, the friend recounted, through those everyday challenges to serve and love your spouse, they started to love each other again.

Then her message continued:

> On September 13, the wife wrote her husband a love letter (which was the challenge for that day) and then she went upstairs to get in bed with him. She woke him up to tell him she had a surprise for him in the morning (this was at 2:00 a.m.) and then asked him if she could hold him. At 4:00 a.m. she accidentally woke him up and said, "Honey, I'm so sorry for waking you up." He said, "Honey, I'm used to it, I love you, goodnight." The next morning he woke up, and she had passed in her sleep.

I was completely floored by the message. In fact, I didn't know what to think or how to feel. But it did seem clear that it was as if God wanted to rekindle their love, provide a beautiful reconciliation, and give the husband a lasting memory of love before the grief came.

Alyssa and I like to say that if your romantic relationship is healthy and flourishing, everything else will be too. But if it's unhealthy and hurtful and not giving life, then it doesn't matter how everything else is doing. In some ways, relationships affect our whole lives. They are the epicenter that ripples out to everything. And this is true even for those who are single and reading this: how we view our relationships, how we trust the Lord in them, and how we walk with Him affects how we live our lives, how we do our jobs, and how we grow.

And that's why we wrote this book. It's not a marriage book, though there is a lot about our marriage in it. It's not a dating book, though we do discuss dating. It's not a sex book either (I mean, what even *is* that?), though we do talk a lot about sexuality in it. We simply wanted to trace our stories and hoped that maybe you'd identify with us in some way. We are in no way perfect or even qualified to write a relationship book. But that's kind of the point. A crooked stick can still draw a straight line, and our marriage, even though it's desperately in need of grace, can hopefully still point you to the place where life, joy, and intimacy is truly found—Jesus.

This book is for the misfits, the broken, the hurt, the tired, the exhausted, the addicted, the divorced, the married, the single, the taken, the seeking, and anyone else hoping to pursue God's vision for all things related to marriage, dating, love, and sexuality.

Because that's our story.

Alyssa had never even held a guy's hand until she held mine when we dated in our twenties. I, on the other hand, lived with the "if it felt good, then do it" motto from the time I entered high school. Yet we both can point to certain parts of our stories that needed deconstructing and that we needed to recover from in some ways—from the downside of the religious purity culture to the ramifications of living without restraint. So in many ways, we want this book to be a third way, one that returns to the Scriptures and asks, "What's God's vision for romantic relationships?"

Because, in our own journey, some of the answers surprised us and have brought incredible joy and life to our marriage. And just like the couple mentioned above, we want to live in a way that when the end comes—when "til death do us part" happens—we can say we lived well, loved well, and pointed to a bigger picture. That our marriage ultimately wasn't about us. That when people saw us, they in some small way got a glimpse of the greatest love—Jesus.

A FEW THINGS TO REMEMBER

Music is, and always has been, a big part of our relationship and has a way of powerfully taking us back to a particular moment, day, or season in our story (including our breakup). A song sometimes has the ability to capture an entire season of your life or sharply feel as if it were specifically written about something in your life. So we thought it'd be fun to replace our chapter titles with titles of songs that we think best sum up the heart of the chapter (some are lyrics, and some are the song titles). Some take a depressing or terrible view of love—but that's the point. We are in no way praising every song listed but are saying that something about the title or in the lyrics deeply resonated with an aspect of the corresponding chapter. You'll probably recognize most of them, but if you want an extra experience, feel free to look them up or have a listen while reading.

As you start reading, you'll notice we took turns writing the chapters. We identify the author of each chapter just to make it a little easier to understand who's writing. I think after a few chapters, though, it'll be clear who you're reading, as we have very different writing styles and communicate differently (which is something we realized about two minutes into our marriage). I (Jeff) like to process big ideas and then break them down. Alyssa tends to process more through storytelling and gentleness. We think it creates a fun dynamic and that we complement each other well. We just hope it's an encouragement to you.

01

WHERE IS THE LOVE?

(The Black Eyed Peas)

I lost my virginity when I was sixteen.

In the back of a car.

In a church parking lot.

To someone who wasn't my girlfriend.

I know that's pretty forward, seeing as how we just met and all. But honestly, I don't say that to shock you. In fact, my intention is quite the opposite. According to stats, *that's normal.*[1]

Oh, and did I mention that Alyssa didn't even hold someone's hand until we started dating in our twenties? To say our marriage was a collision of two very different stories would be an understatement. But that's Alyssa's story, and I'll let her tell it in subsequent chapters.

When I think back to that time in my life, I shudder. I was plagued with debilitating insecurity, trying so hard to fit the mold projected as necessary to be popular. Isn't it interesting how much we sacrifice simply in hopes that others will like us and think we are cool?

I was searching—and searching desperately. I wanted to be liked, I wanted to be accepted. I wanted to be *known.* But from the outside I looked like a model kid. I was on the high school baseball team that played in two state championships in a row. My teachers usually told my mom that I was very bright but that I could probably apply myself a little more. I was the guy who seemed to have it all together. I spent an exhausting amount of energy on editing and protecting my image and caring about what others thought of me. And when you spend all your time on that, you have no time for anything else—yourself, your passions, your joy, following Jesus, and so on.

Filtering your life, or having others believe a lie about you (or at least a half-truth), is a full-time job.

I now see more clearly just how dark a time that was for me. If you were able to ask sixteen-year-old Jeff if he thought it was a dark time, I'm sure he'd say no. But that's because I had nothing to compare it to. I thought being paralyzed by shame and guilt, not knowing what I was created for, and living for others' approval was normal. That thinking culminated in a poor view of love, sexuality, and women that resulted in a string of terrible and unhealthy relationships and making bad decisions for years. And I'm still working through the ramifications of that today. High school was ground zero in many ways—the place where I began to make decisions that crashed in on me later.

We may not realize it, but many of us are playing a game of emotional and spiritual Jenga when it comes to romance, sexuality, and love. We make a lot of decisions that feel good in the moment, that seem like good ideas at the time, before we even consider their consequences. And just like in Jenga, every poor decision we make is another piece we remove from the tower, weakening our wholeness and humanness.

Most likely, it will all come crashing down. After a terrible breakup. An unhealthy relationship. Heartache. Fierce anger and bitterness.

It's only *then* we realize it was the little decisions along the way that brought us to that point. The reason the breakup hurt so bad in college was because we set up unhealthy relationship patterns when we were fifteen. The reason our marriage starts to lose its foundation is that in our dating relationships in college we moved on to the next person as soon as the butterflies went away.
The reason we almost cracked under the weight of shame after having sex with our boyfriend or girlfriend is because we spent years placing our identity not in Jesus but in purity rings and "true love waits" bracelets.

When we were actually making those decisions, nothing fell on our heads in those moments, so we thought we were in the clear. When we pulled a piece out of the tower, everything still held together.

When we said "just this once" and clicked on that link to watch porn.

When we went to that party and made out with that person we never saw again.

When we fantasized about that girl or made up a whole scenario of life with that guy who wasn't ours to think about in the first place.

When we stayed in the relationship even when all our friends and family said not to.

When we led that guy or girl on because we wanted to have control or feel wanted, even though we didn't really like them enough to date them.

So we kept going. We kept doing it.

Until one day, one particular decision became that final piece of Jenga—right when it was removed, it all fell apart. A pile at our feet.

I got married in my early twenties and quickly realized how those decisions and views and thoughts from ages ago were staring me in the face. I was fighting an uphill battle, one that was on a ninety-degree cliff.

I don't think I'm alone in that feeling.

In fact, I'm a decade removed from that season in my life, and sometimes it feels like yesterday. There are images. Hundreds of images. Dozens of memories.

Burned into the front of my brain.

And in some ways, I'm still haunted by those pictures and memories and thoughts. Sometimes following Jesus is gritty—blood, sweat, and tears type of stuff. There are moments when an uninvited, shameful memory jumps right in front of my concentration, and it takes everything in me—usually me lying on the floor, gritting my teeth, hands on my head—to remind myself of truth and ask: *What does God say about me in this moment? What does He say about Himself right now?*

That sixteen-year-old Jeff is dead. He was left in the grave, was nailed to the same cross Jesus was, the minute I said yes to following Him. I'm a new creation. Shame has been defeated. Jesus looks at me with searing, white-hot, ferocious love. I'm His.

This is the battleground of a healthy relationship: *the mind*. It starts there. Our thoughts can define us, and right views of God are the most important things about us because they create the entire trajectory of our lives.

•

Alyssa and I have battled with thoughts that harm our relationship. The way we see it, both of us came into our marriage sick in some way. A disease of sorts had been coursing through our systems for most of our lives, but sometimes it takes a marriage to start seeing the symptoms.

It reminds me of a party we had before we moved from Washington to Maui. We didn't know it at the time, but someone was definitely carrying a crazy intense virus. Within three days of the party, eleven of the fourteen people came down with a stomach bug that involved being wrapped around a toilet for two days straight, not knowing what end it was going to come out of next (and if you've been there, you know that might be one of the worst predicaments you can ever face in life).

When I was at the party, I didn't *feel* sick. I didn't *feel* like I caught anything. I didn't *feel* infected. In fact, I felt just the opposite. Happy, cheery, hanging out with friends and family. It wasn't until many days later that I actually *was* sick.

Yet, I had *caught* the virus at the party days earlier.

In many ways, that's us with love.

We are lovesick and love-diseased. Our views of romance, sexuality, dating, and marriage are killing us. We've been infected for years and haven't even realized it. It almost killed me in high school and stayed with me in college, like shrapnel in my soul that I'm still plucking out and finding healing for. Nothing has caused me more pain, grief, and hurt than previous relationships and my pursuit of love.

Isn't that true for most of us? We get to our midtwenties or midthirties and feel like we should be *beginning* our adult lives, yet it feels more like the end. We are tired. We are hurt. We are exhausted. And we don't want to do it anymore. We are left to pick up the pieces of our adolescence, and we now look back with enough perspective to realize just how detrimental our decisions have been.

How did we get here? Why are so many of us entering adult life, our marriages, jobs, and new families hanging on by a thread rather than starting our journey with vibrancy and life and fullness?

Maybe it has something to do with our bad definition of love.

Clearly something isn't working. Clearly we've got some wires crossed.

Our culture at large is hurt. Sick. Unhealthy. Bruised. Broken.

And a question that haunts me is, if we are *all* sick, do we realize how sick we truly are?

Loneliness has been declared an epidemic.[2]

Porn has gotten so out of control, it's been labeled a "public health crisis" and "public hazard," as Pamela Anderson, one of the most famous porn stars in history, put it.[3]

The use of antidepressants has more than doubled since 1998.[4]

"Friends with benefits" and "no strings attached" seem to be the normative view of most relationships—and of Hollywood movie titles.

Marriage is becoming so trivial, or is failing at such a high rate, that some lawmakers have considered things like a "two-year marriage license" instead of a lifetime commitment.[5]

And selfish, casual, hookup sex has reached its logical conclusion in many ways. It has been so detached from an actual relationship that some people now buy lifelike robots that they can customize and have sex with.[6] *I mean, if sex is simply about pleasuring yourself and getting what you want out of it, then why not get a robot instead of another human? They are much easier, and always "in the mood" as long as they're plugged in.*

In a strange irony, one of the biggest pornography sites in the world, a place that is probably the farthest from real love, since you are literally having sex with yourself while staring at a computer screen, seems to be full of people in search of that very thing, as the most frequently used word in its comments section is *love*.[7]

Loneliness. Trivial marriages. Sex robots. Porn.

In a world where you can get anything you want at any time (as long as you have Amazon Prime or Postmates), love seems to be the proverbial carrot on a stick.

Yet Scripture says that "God is love."

And a famous quote says, "Every man who knocks on the door of a brothel is looking for God."

The good news is that the reverse is also true. God is knocking on the door of every brothel, looking for man. We all have our different brothels—places we go in search of connection, intimacy, and love. We need to be in a relationship because we are addicted to approval and that feeling of emotional and relational intimacy.

For some, it's the need to be recognized, liked, affirmed, and admired.

Or we scratch our heads, wondering why we so easily fall in and out of love with people we are dating, not realizing we are addicted to an ideal of a person who doesn't exist, and our ideal not only crushes them but also doesn't satisfy us. Then we move on, hoping to find it with the next person, creating a vicious cycle.

We become human bodies full of wounds, hurts, emotions, and scars, carrying around so much baggage that we aren't sure how much farther we can go. But what if it wasn't actually love that got us to that place? What if it was the misunderstanding of love that did?

•

When I was sixteen and fresh out of driver's ed, I had my first flat tire. I say "first," because, well, let's just say my first couple of years behind the wheel didn't go so well. (If we ever have coffee, remind me to tell you about that one time I totaled my first car after only owning it for two weeks because I thought it would be a good idea to hydroplane *purposely* in big puddles for fun—with the car my dad had spent months building and repairing before giving it to me.)

I remember driving and feeling like something was a little off in the car's movement. I was a few miles from home, driving on a side street after hanging out with some friends. (I can't remember exactly what I was listening to but knowing the year, it was probably "Yeah" by Usher or "Boulevard of Broken Dreams" by Green Day. I may have an eclectic taste in music.) But it felt like the gas wasn't working or that the emergency brake was on or the gas pedal needed to be pressed a little harder than usual to stay at a normal speed. It felt like I was towing or dragging something.

Since this was my first flat tire, I didn't know what it was. I thought a flat tire would be more obvious. You know, like in the movies, where a tire explodes and the car spins out of control. At least in my case, driving felt off and weird, but I could still accelerate, turn, and stop.

Little did I know that every second I drove with a flat tire, the worse it was for my whole car—the rims, the engine, the alignment, and more. But I kept driving. And my car kept getting worse and worse and worse.

For a lot of us, the way we see love, dating, sexuality, marriage, and romance is like a flat tire. There's a little something off at first. We know it and we feel it. Sure, we can still get from point A to point B on a flat tire. Sure, it does the job. Sure, sex before marriage doesn't feel wrong. Sure, living together while you're dating helps you learn more about each other. But there are moments when it feels "off." There are moments when it feels more damaging than it should. But we don't know any better, so we keep driving. And it gets worse. And worse. And worse.

We were created for more.

We were never meant to drive on a flat tire. We were never meant to have sex with someone who wasn't our husband or wife. We were never meant to be addicted to porn. We were never meant to be so wrapped up in a relationship that makes us feel as if we are losing our god when we break up with that boyfriend or girlfriend.

Years later, when we finally pull over to look under the hood, many of us realize—for the first time—just how damaging the flat tire was.

The compounded years have made us view love as something we can take instead of what we can receive.

As something we feel instead of something to commit to.

The reason love, romance, and sexuality feel so right, even when they are wrong, is because we were created for them. Even the distortions hold an element of truth; that's what a distortion is—an alteration of the original. But there's more. So much more. God doesn't want to take away our joy; He wants to give us more of it. He doesn't want to take away our sexual desire; He wants to give us the context in which it works the best. God doesn't want us to hate romance; He wants to introduce us to the greatest love story of all time.

In order to realize where we went so wrong, we first need to see where it was all so right. Where this intoxicating intimacy and love comes from in the first place.

•

As author Christopher West says, "Love, by its nature, desires to expand its own communion."[8] God didn't need us. He was perfectly complete in and of Himself. But love creates. Love overflows. Love is abundance. Love is life. God made it so, simply out of the goodness of who He is, that He would create image bearers to share in that beautiful exchange of love. A beautiful picture of otherness becoming oneness. That's what marriage vows mean. That's what sex is in body. And that's what covenant is in promise.

We can't miss the truth found in that beautiful divine and mysterious and glorious moment. That when He created us and all the uniqueness of male and female bodies, He was choosing to communicate something about Himself.

One of the first commands in all Scripture is to have sex. Well, God's exact words are "be fruitful and multiply" (Genesis 1:28),

LOVE CREATES. LOVE OVERFLOWS. LOVE IS ABUNDANCE. LOVE IS LIFE.

but you get the idea. Because even before sin entered the world, male and female were incomplete and were built with a longing, a holy longing for the otherness to become oneness. That's the story we were created to tell.

As the poet Wendell Berry put it, "The sexuality of community life is centered on marriage, which joins two living souls as closely as, in this world, they can be joined. This joining of two who know, love, and trust one another brings them in the same breath in the freedom of sexual consent and into the fullest earthly realization of the image of God. From their joining, other living souls come into being, and with them great responsibilities that are unending, fearful, and joyful."[9]

It's striking to me how often sexuality and the Christian religion face off as enemies in various cultures, when in reality, nothing or no one has a more dynamic, powerful, beautiful, weighty, and incredible view of sexuality than the follower of Jesus does. That very moment when husband and wife come together in perfect love—not only in Spirit and in soul, but also in their bodies—is one of the clearest pictures we have of God. It's telling a story.

And God created our bodies so that we could partake in that story. Sexuality. Male. And female. That we might be "other" but come together as one. That there might be a communion of persons and an exchange of love. That when brought together, they produce a "third" image.

In the first couple of words of Scripture (Genesis 1:1), an assumption is made: "In the beginning, God created the heavens and the earth," which implies that before those things were created, God still was, and is, and is to come. He was there before anything. And immediately we get a hint as well at the divine mystery that is the Trinity. He says, "Let *us* make man in our image" (Genesis 1:26), implying a plurality, yet at the same time we see the obvious singularity of this Creator.

It takes a while for the scriptures to fully unpack this beautiful truth, but as they do so we can read backward and see from that very moment God is and always has been an endless cycle and circle of love. The perfect picture of three persons yet oneness—the Father, the Son, and the very Spirit of God—eternally surrendering and submitting and exalting one another. So when God says let Us make man in Our image in Genesis 1, that means humans are born out of the overflow of God's very own image. We are born out of *that*. And whatever we are created *out of*, also is what we were created *for*.

At its core, sexuality is an expression of the mystery of the Trinity. An opportunity to tell the greatest story ever told: that somehow there is more than one, yet somehow there is one.

Our bodies are telling this story.

This is why children and marriage are meant to happen together. Marriage is two becoming one; children are born out of the overflow of love and oneness. They are image bearers. They are mini images that the love created.

Of course, things don't always happen how they should. We must face the fact that we are born into a curse-stricken world.

Infertility. Broken marriages. Even the deaths of children. Yet there is so much grace and so much healing in Jesus for all of us.

In fact, I think the reason infertility is so painful is that our souls echo, *This isn't how it should be.* And as Scripture shows us, *how it should be* can also teach us about how it is.

Our love yearns for an outlet. For an overflow. In Scripture it's clear that Jesus is in the business of redemption, of new creation, and of telling His story. That happens every day in two-parent homes, one-parent homes, infertile homes, adoptive homes, homes that have suffered miscarriages, and so on.

For some, that overflow of love carries over into work. Notice how God Himself was eternal love first, and then He created. The endless love of God bubbled up into earth and heaven and skies and moon and sun and animals and ultimately us. Creation was born *out* of love.

Yet our culture also idolizes work. Too many people exhaust themselves and sacrifice their families and marriages in the process. But godly work flows *from* the covenant of love. Not the other way around. In Scripture, marriage is an overflow of love. It is no coincidence that the Bible begins and ends with a marriage.

Adam and Eve in Genesis.

Jesus and His church in Revelation.

If you could summarize the Bible succinctly, it would be about God creating, looking for, pursuing, and restoring a bride. A people for Himself. To be called into that oneness.

It's why all the love stuff—those butterflies, dating, romance, marriage, intimacy, sex, and that deep connection you feel when you're both vulnerable and fully loved at the same time—is not about us. In the end, we are just reflections.

•

A couple of years ago, I had the opportunity to travel to Morocco and be on the set during a week of shooting for the production of a huge TV show that would air during prime time on NBC later that year. To say it was as big as it gets is an understatement. They built lifelike sets in the middle of the desert. I remember the distinct feeling of awe and amazement I experienced all week. It felt surreal not only to be on a set larger than life, but also to peek behind the curtain and see just how they make movie and TV magic. It was incredible.

My friend who traveled with me and I got to hang out in a tent where we wore headphones connected to all the other audio sets (the director, the actors, and so on). One of my favorite things was listening to the director do his job. When I watch shows on TV, I only see the final product, but being there on set, I got to look behind the scenes to the *why*. I got to see why the director had those characters stand there and say their lines with a particular intonation, and why he chose that camera angle—all to further the story.

I remember thinking, *That's exactly what marriage is like.* It's a peek behind the curtain. It's the Creator of the universe coming down to us at the wedding ceremony and whispering, "Hey, you want to know what I'm like? You want to know how I love? You want to know how I relate to you as humans? Here ya go. Here's your picture."

And that's why ultimately love in us is only a reflection of the true thing. Like those actors on the set, or me as a kid when I put on my Superman outfit, we are pointing to a reality, but we are not the reality itself. In those moments it's real, but it's not the ultimate reality, which is why when we are fully joined in union with God at the end of time, there will be no marriages. You don't need the shadow when the real thing is in front of you.

And that's God with us. His love is the reality. His ferocious pursuit of us is the real thing. Our job is to reflect His love back to Him. And in marriage and romance and sexuality, we get to learn what that means. We get to learn what it means to love unconditionally. What it means to pursue no matter what. What it means to forgive endlessly. What it means to serve without condition.

I distinctly remember a little whisper in my soul when I was sixteen years old in the back of that car in the church parking lot. I knew what we were doing wasn't it. That wasn't what I was created for. I was telling a lie. With my body. And with my life. But it took me years to fully realize that and pick up the pieces.

In that particular season of my life, I came to recognize that sex could not "deliver the goods."

While cheap sex might not be what you are exchanging for true love, many of us often put something else in its place.

A feeling.

A fairy tale.

A substance.

Disillusionment.

Serial relationships.

But those aren't love. And great love takes effort and commitment and lots of time—because it's in those things that the depth and beauty and mystery of a true love will show itself superior to the false realities, the lesser reflections we cheapen it with.

TAKEAWAY

Before God's vision for healthy relationships can fully develop, we have to detox from poor, harmful, and parodied versions of love, sex, marriage, and dating.

02

WHAT MAKES
YOU BEAUTIFUL

(One Direction)

I had an eating disorder for six years. Anorexia was the name of my game. I never threw up; I couldn't bring myself to do it. And it never got so bad that I had to be put in a rehab center. But it plagued me for years. You never would have known. I mean, you may have known if you were familiar with eating disorders, and if you spent any time with me during mealtimes. But I loved Jesus. I was a leader in the church and on my school campus. I prayed, I read God's Word, and I trusted Him. And yet when it came to my body, somehow I'd separated it from my soul. Or so I thought. In reality, that separation was destructive to myself and to others. It wreaked havoc on my heart, my mind, and my soul, and it broke others' hearts around me.

It's so easy to compare our bodies to other women's bodies—especially those of celebrities and others on social media.

Why can't I look like them?

Why can't I lose the weight like she did?

How does she do it?

It's nothing new. Same struggle. Same lies being thrown at us. And we have to fight our thoughts. For me, that's daily. I daily have to turn it over to the Lord. I daily have to tell myself the truth of who I am in Him and that God's truth prevails. Yeah, I do want to get rid of some of these pregnancy rolls. But the truth is that God loves me, that He gave me a body to live in—not to starve. Or to diet to death. And now more than ever, I realize that how I view food and my body affects others.

The other day I was walking my dog and pushing my five-month-old in a stroller, and I caught myself starting to open that dark door again. *I just want to lose some weight around my middle. And my thighs. And my butt. I'll walk now. Then tomorrow I'll do my workout videos. Maybe I should cut out sweets? Or just add some vegetables at dinner? Maybe no more eating out—*

No!

"No, I won't do this. I'm not going there. Lord, I need You."

I stopped and cried out to God. No, I wasn't going to go down that path. I wasn't going to start planning my food for the rest of the day, or put myself through a strict plan, or give into the lies about areas of my body I don't like and wish were different. That's exactly what Satan wanted me to do, but I knew it was toxic. That wouldn't lead to life, but rather to death.

In 2 Corinthians 12 Paul talks about how he pleaded with God to remove a thorn in his flesh several times, but God didn't do it. We don't know what Paul's thorn was. Paul calls it a "messenger of Satan to harass me." Why in the world would God not remove it? Paul was crying out, pleading with God to remove something that was not of Him.

Eating, along with my body image, is one of my thorns in the flesh. That and anxiety. Super fun, right? This is my thing. Not to say that I don't sin and struggle in other ways, because I totally do. But eating and my body image, and all that goes along with it, often seems to be a struggle for me. I'm not identified by my past eating disorder, but it is a big part of my story that still affects me. I may always struggle in this area, but God has brought healing and freedom in this area of my life, and I continue to grow in it daily.

I can agree with Paul that God says, "'My grace is sufficient for you, for my power is made perfect in weakness.' Therefore, I will boast all the more gladly of my weaknesses, so that the power of Christ may rest upon me" (2 Corinthians 12:9–10).

My awareness of how easily I could fall into this trap again makes me rely on His grace, and it makes me empathetic toward other women who struggle with the same thing. I won't tell you to just get over it, because I know it's not something you "just get over." I get it. I'm right there with you. I'm clinging to God's grace and power, and that's all I have. But it's sufficient.

He's right there with me.

He is the Victor.

My hope is in Him.

Identity plays a huge part in our relationships. How you view yourself will flow into every relationship you have, especially a romantic one. Often guys wonder, *Am I good enough?* and girls wonder, *Am I worthy?* If those questions aren't rooted in Jesus and what He says about you, then they can bring some heavy baggage into a relationship. They can cause you to feel like you constantly have to prove yourself, or devastate you when you mess up or fail. They can cause you to be manipulative or clingy, or perhaps even lead to an eating disorder. What questions do you ask yourself late into the night, and what answers are you feeding your soul? Lies? Or truth?

•

I grew up in a home with two parents who love each other immensely. My dad worked hard to provide for us and spent his off hours and days playing with me and helping around the house. He brought joy and laughter to our home, always thinking of the next joke to tell us. He's faithful, gentle, and sweet. My mom always supported my dad. She honored him with her words and treated him like a king when he got home from work. She always made every celebration special, created a home that was a refuge, and was constantly pursuing my heart.

I've always felt secure in my parents' love for me and in their love for each other. In fact, I remember, when I was about six, my dad sitting down with me and promising that he and my mom would never divorce. That promise brought such comfort to my young heart, and they still choose each other daily.

HOW YOU VIEW YOURSELF WILL FLOW INTO EVERY RELATIONSHIP YOU HAVE, ESPECIALLY A ROMANTIC ONE.

When I was a little older, I asked my parents how they met and fell in love. I've asked them a million times since then because I just love hearing their story. I love hearing new little insights each time they tell it, hearing them interrupt each other with playful smiles, somehow each one always having a little different take on the story.

My dad was in his late twenties, working as a baker at a restaurant. One day my mom, who was the new waitress, walked in the door, and he instantly knew she was the woman he wanted to marry. My mom, however, was not so convinced. They went on a date, but according to my mom, she did not want to spend forever with him. So my dad entered the friend zone. They saw each other at work, lived in the same apartment complex, and hung out with the same circle of friends.

A year went by, and they went on a ski trip with their friends. Well, magic happened on that trip, and they came back as a couple. (Cue the sappy music and fireworks.) They dated for a while. Then my dad moved to another state to start up a restaurant. He was working from sunup to sundown, without many days off. My mom went out to see him and barely got to hang out with him because he was working so much. Dad broke up with her, saying he wanted to marry her but honestly didn't know when he'd have enough time off during the next two years to marry her.

Two weeks after that, my dad asked himself, *What in the world did I just do? This is crazy to choose a job over the woman I love!* So he quit his job, flew to California, and proposed to my mom.

Growing up in such a secure and loving home, I deeply desired the same thing. I wanted to be loved and pursued by a man, to do life with him, to have a family. (When I was five, I was a bride for Halloween!) Ever since preschool, I've had crushes on boys. I would write love notes and give them to my current crush on the school bus.

I remember trying to kiss my first "boyfriend" behind the famous rock that sat in the yard near our elementary school's playground. The rock was useful for playing hide-and-seek, for climbing on, and apparently for hiding behind and kissing! I remember our friends circled around us. I was wearing heavy bubble gum lip balm, and my boyfriend and I were so uncoordinated that we completely missed each other's lips!

I talked for hours on the phone with the boy I currently liked and would take a century to write just the right thing in my crush's yearbook. I saw the love my parents had and wanted the same thing.

But as I grew older and no boys pursued me, my hopes and dreams of that type of love faded. My friends were all dating, being asked to dances, and having their first kisses. But no one was lined up for my affection.

I started to compare myself with the girls who were dating. It seemed like all of them were thin and beautiful, bubbly, athletic, or musical. They all had something going for them.

•

When I began following God the summer before my freshman year of high school, I realized that life was all about Him, not me. I became more reserved and quiet after that. I didn't really put myself out there when it came to guys. I loved languages and was good at school. I loved interacting one-on-one with people, too, but none of that necessarily made me stand out to guys.

I know now that I could have kept my bubbly personality while still pointing to Jesus, but when I became a sophomore in high school, I thought I had to act and be a certain way. I took aerobics as an elective and loved it. Then I got really sick for a couple of weeks and lost a lot of weight. I liked my new size and started to notice other girls in my aerobics class talking about their weight and how to lose pounds. I quickly caught on and soon became very aware of how much I weighed.

I began to obsess with what number on the scale to target. It was fun to lose weight every week and to have to go shopping for new clothes because the ones I owned were too big. I started to think that beauty equaled being thin. *Surely my new size will attract a guy,* I thought.

As the months wore on, my "perfect" size kept getting smaller and smaller. A size six became a four, which became a two. I loved working out and started to think of creative ways to eat less and less. I didn't starve myself completely and my obsession wasn't totally overwhelming, but soon what became a desire to look beautiful and maybe turn a guy's eye became a control issue for me.

Whenever something in my life was difficult or hard, something that I had no control over, I turned to food. Or, rather, my goal was to avoid food. It became the one thing in my life that I could control.

Hard test coming up? Watch what you eat.

Conflict with a friend? Cut back on carbs.

Not sure which college to attend? No sugar.

Heartbroken over a crush? Salads only.

I would turn to Jesus and pray and seek Him, I would ask for His help and surrender, but as soon as I finished praying, I would form a game plan in my head of what to eat and what not to eat. I longed for control.

My best friend would always tell me to eat more. She was concerned about me. And my parents started to encourage me to eat too. They could see an unhealthy habit forming in me, but I just shrugged it off. *It's really not that big of a deal.* I didn't see how it was slowly destroying me.

This went on for six years—two years in high school, and it flowed into my whole college career. In fact, when I went to college, it got worse. For the first time, I was away from all my family and friends who loved and cared for me. I was on my own. I made new friends. Friends who didn't know my past or my struggles. I wasn't coming home to home-cooked meals anymore, and I could choose what to eat and what not to eat. I could even take the food to go, so no one really knew how much, or how little, I was eating. It was only between me and God, and although there was a check in my heart, I didn't think what I was doing was really that bad.

On the outside, I was this girl who loved Jesus. And I did really love Jesus. I woke up every morning with my coffee in hand to read my Bible. I would go running and pour out my heart to Him. I was an RA (resident assistant) and taught girls in Bible studies. I led a missions group to South Africa. But on the inside, I was slowly dying. I felt so alone. Like no one really knew me. They didn't know my thoughts. The thoughts that taunted me almost every hour.

You're fat.

Your thighs are too big.

Can't you have a stomach like that girl?

Look at her arms; they're perfect.

No cookies today.

Maybe I can just have an apple and some toast for dinner tonight.

I compared myself with every girl I saw. How did I measure up? I woke up in the morning with my first thought being about what I would eat that day, and I planned out every meal. It wasn't about counting calories anymore. It was more about how little I could eat. I didn't tell anyone about my hellish thoughts. I couldn't. I didn't want them to know that I wasn't perfect, or rather that I actually had a huge problem. I mean, I was a leader on campus; how could I tell anyone my very real problems?

I remember one day walking up a hill to my dorm after lunch. I had a container in my hand that held an apple and an English muffin. It was a bright sunny day, and yet my heart was dark and cold. With tears streaming down my face, I was once again planning what I was going to eat that day. I couldn't get it off my mind. I couldn't stop. I felt like I was in a dark dungeon, crying to get out, with my arms flailing out the prison window, but no one could hear me. No one could save me. I was stuck. And the room was getting darker and darker.

My best friend was the only person who really knew my struggle. I didn't tell her everything, but she knew. She could see it and would actually ask me about it. And she kept asking. She cared, deeply. She prayed for me and loved me through it. She would cry with me over it but was never judgmental or harsh. She showed me truth and grace and compassion. Before I left for a summer internship in Maui, I spent a weekend with her. She asked how I was doing, and I told her everything. It had gotten worse. My body was weak and frail because I was starving it. She told me she was praying I would find a mentor after I moved to Maui, someone who would help me with this. Someone I could talk to, who would walk me through it.

And the Lord did just that. He brought two ladies into my life who immediately knew. They didn't need to ask. They loved me well and made space for me to talk and be open. For the first time since my sophomore year of high school, I was ready to be open and talk about it. I had gone to the doctor shortly after moving to Maui, and the doctor had looked at me and told me I was too thin.

For some reason, that broke me. Finally. After all those years of trying to appear perfect on the outside, of stuffing this struggle down, of not letting anyone into my darkness, of carrying this heavy load, I finally was done. Tears poured out. I was broken. I realized that what I was doing was a sin. It didn't please the Lord; in fact, it deeply hurt Him. I was consumed with my outward appearance and trying to control so many things in my life, instead of truly resting in Him.

I had believed the lies constantly thrown at me about who I was and who I should be.

You're not beautiful.

You're not worthy of a guy's affection.

You can control things.

You should be a size ____.

You're all alone.

There's no escaping.

I was done. I wanted freedom. I wanted to be fully known, to be okay with not having it all together. To understand that I was loved anyway. I wanted to be healed. To have my mind set free from my consuming thoughts, and to think on things that were true and right and lovely. I wanted to truly trust God. To know who I am in His eyes.

I told one of my roommates that same day of my eating disorder. She just held my hand and told me it would be okay. We'd get through it together. And we did. My roommates were just who I needed. Three beautiful girls who didn't care about counting calories or watching what you ate. That was a foreign concept to them. They all loved food and loved to eat. Something I grew to love as well.

I asked one of my mentors for help, and God knew I needed her. She had gone through the exact same thing in high school and understood my struggle. She not only prayed with me but also helped me on a practical level. She kept me accountable. She asked me what I had eaten each day and either called me out or cheered me on. She taught me what a healthy meal looked like. My idea of food and portions was so distorted at that point that I needed someone to teach me what to eat, and how much, all over again.

And then I told my boss, a youth pastor. While it was hard for me to tell a guy about it, he needed to know that I struggled in this area. He sat down with me and was so kind and compassionate. He told me that eating disorders for girls can be likened to porn for guys. Both are an addiction. Both a mind game. Both personal and can be kept secret. The way that guys struggle with lust is similar to how girls are always thinking about food. Somehow, that brought hope to my heart. I knew I wasn't alone in it and that there could be healing and freedom.

Things certainly didn't change overnight, but slowly the struggle eased up. Slowly I learned what God says about me and clung to His truth, not my own distorted views. I realized that I was formed in His image, that I was made with purpose and goodness and beauty. I reflected God.

I clung to the truth that God formed me in my mother's womb, and I was fearfully and wonderfully made. He knew me and loved every part of me. Every part of my body was made by Him. He didn't leave it to chance or look away or forget about a certain part. No, he made each part intentionally. He wanted me to have brown hair and green eyes. He gave me thighs that were perfect for me, no matter what their size, so that I could hike, run, and paddleboard. He gave me a bigger bottom because, well, I'm sure there are other reasons, but one of them is that Jeff loves it.

And I learned that the Holy Spirit lives inside me; I'm His temple. Therefore I need to take care of this body that He's given me. In our Christian culture, it's easy to buy into the philosophy that our bodies are separate from our spirit and perhaps aren't "spiritual." But we're connected. My body, spirit, and soul are all connected, and each affects the other. My whole being is spiritual.

If I don't take care of my body and I feed it crap and sit on the couch all day, most likely I'll get depressed and feel purposeless. If I have sex with someone who isn't my spouse, my soul and spirit will be connected to that person, regardless of how much I tell myself it's no big deal. In sex, two become one. It's how God created it. And if I'm starving my body, my spirit can't be set free. It's all interconnected and it all matters. And I need to take care of my physical body, just as much as I take care of my spirit and soul.

I thought for so many years that if I was a certain size, and if I had control over my life in this area, some guy would come knocking on my door. But rather, for me, it was the opposite. It was when I finally laid it all down and started to walk in freedom that the guy came into my life. I was so thankful to be on the journey of healing when I started dating, to know that true beauty was in how Jesus saw me, not in some guy's opinion. Jesus was my security, and my identity was in *Him*.

I see now, however, that God had the perfect plan for my healing. Jeff was a vital part of my story. His love, compassion, and tender heart made me realize how much it really did hurt my Father's heart when I didn't see myself the way He sees me, and how beautiful wholeness can be. Being skinny on the outside and tortured on the inside was hell. But being healthy and strong on the outside, and free and full of grace on the inside was just how God intended it.

TAKEAWAY

We are not identified by our pasts, but our pasts continue to affect us. They are part of our stories. Our outward appearance is not our identity. The truth is, we were each formed in God's image and created with purpose and goodness and beauty. We reflect God. Our hope is in Him.

03

SLOW DANCING IN A BURNING ROOM

(John Mayer)

I distinctly remember the first time I looked at a girl *that way*. When I didn't see her as a person, but as an object. When I didn't see someone as a whole, but as someone whose parts were more important than her person.

I was ten, standing with my buddies in the hallway of my middle school. (Quick sidenote: I skipped a grade in elementary school, so I was a lot younger than my peers. Add to that, my birthday is in June, which is at the end of the school year, so some kids in my grade were almost two years older than I was. There's a big difference between a twelve- or thirteen-year-old and a ten-year-old when it comes to hormones and puberty.) A girl walked by us, and my friend made a comment about her body. By the way he said it and what he said, it was clear this was common talk among the guys. I honestly remember being confused. I didn't get it. My mind and body and hormones didn't think like that yet. There was a disconnect.

But I also felt as if in that moment a doorway opened up. I had a funny feeling I couldn't quite place, because it was a feeling I had never had before. I remember partly feeling dirty and partly enjoying it. It was strange for me, at ten years old, to feel something wake in me that I hadn't known was there. And I think this is one of evil's biggest tools: getting to us before we have a framework for or concept of what's going on. In my case, not realizing until ten years later what was going on.

When our lives crash and burn in our twenties or thirties and our marriages fall apart, we wonder how we got there. We begin digging into our souls for answers and healing, and searching for help like people feeling around in a dark room for the light switch. I peeled layer after layer in search of a solution, only to find a ten-year-old boy, a naked woman, and a computer screen looking back at me. It's easy to get pushed into a cage if you don't know that's not a place you should go.

So in my story, that was the year—the ripe old age of ten—that I began my apprenticeship.

Of course, we'd usually not call it an apprenticeship, but that's exactly what it is. The truth is, we all learn about life somewhere. And in my case, with no dad at home, I had to look elsewhere.

This is just how the world works. Someone or something is driving you. Someone or something is your teacher. And so we grow up mimicking those who came before us. Trying to be cool or to fit in or to be like those just a little bit ahead of us, only to realize that they've been doing the same thing you are. We might even get to an age when we realize the cycle and want to break it yet end up right where we started.

For example, I grew up in a lower-income neighborhood, where fatherlessness was the norm, not the exception. It was a rarity to have a friend who would share stories of football or going on camping trips with his dad. When I saw friends playing catch with their dads at the park, there was a small sense of envy (even though my mom could throw as well as any of the dads!). As years went by, I'd see kids who resented their dads for abandoning their families and vowed to never be like that, to never grow up and turn out to be the same shadows of a dad. The kids would get to their teenage years and have kids of their own and then take off. The very same thing their dads did. A perpetual cycle.

Fatherlessness taught boys like me about life. We heard about sex from our friends. Saw porn for the first time on a buddy's phone in the PE locker room. And then some boys turn nineteen and find that they're dads but decide they don't want the responsibility. Then they leave the moms to raise their children all by themselves. They vow to never be like their fathers, but it's too late—they already are.

•

While my amazing mom worked like crazy to provide a roof over my head and clothes on my back—in fact, she was pretty much a supermom—even she'd admit she could only do so much. With no father figure at home, she was fighting an uphill battle. MTV, boys a few years older than me, locker rooms full of my teammates, and whatever I saw in advertisements and culture became my teachers. They showed me how to treat women. How to look at women. How to be a man. What I needed to aspire to. What I needed to be like.

Looking back, I see how this dramatically shaped my view of women and relationships. I was unable to process this out loud as a young boy, and once I became a teenager, it became awkward to talk about with my mom, as is the case with many teenage boys. So I grabbed onto whatever looked the best or felt the best. Self-control, discipline, and delay of gratification weren't things that were very esteemed in the messages I was getting from culture. In fact, I heard what sounded like the opposite: Whatever you want, you can have. Take it. It can be yours.

Without any father figure in your teenage years, trying to learn what it means to be a man is like trying to run a marathon as a toddler. You simply won't be able to. And you weren't created to. We were created to learn and be discipled and mentored by those who came before us. Culturally this is true across the board. Boys best learn to be men and husbands and fathers from their own fathers' examples.

Even though you may not realize it, having the example of your parents' loving and healthy marriage has a profound impact on you. Tens of thousands of micro moments and conversations and chances to watch your mom and dad love and serve each other amid their problems and baggage add up to thousands of hours. Showing you what it takes. Showing you what it looks like.

I didn't have that. And it's obvious from stats that I'm not alone. On average, one in four kids under eighteen are in fatherless homes.[1]

So for me, love became simply about taking. About getting what I wanted. About using.

And what I thought was love, was no love at all.

A couple of years ago, one of the most popular songs on the radio was a song called "Black Widow." The opening lyric is about loving someone until they hate you. And that's the type of love I learned—a distorted, cheap, knockoff version.

The relationships I had been in were toxic. Relationships were my drug, and I was an addict. Have you ever been there? Where everything in you knows it's a terrible relationship, but you keep returning. You go to that person for worth, satisfaction, and identity—things another person can never give you. And the longer you're in the relationship, the harder it is to get out. You have moments of seething anger, yet minutes later, you are making up. And the truth is, it's an idolatrous love. The other person has become someone you worship. Not just someone you're dating. Your boyfriend or girlfriend is your golden calf.

Idolatrous love is less like love and more like choking on smoke. When you're choking, you start scratching and ripping for anything that can save you. And that's what those relationships feel like. Idolatrous love is fumes. Real love is oxygen. One gives you death. One gives you life. One is lust. One is love.

When our love is an idolatrous love, we usually define ourselves and find our identity in the relationship. If we don't have the relationship, we are nothing. We have no reason to live and no purpose. We are setting ourselves up for failure if our significant others are *everything* to us.

WE ARE SETTING OURSELVES UP FOR FAILURE IF OUR SIGNIFICANT OTHERS ARE *EVERYTHING* TO US.

Alyssa and I agreed long ago that we aren't looking for each
other to be our everything. We both want a spouse who loves
Jesus more than us. When Jesus is your everything, you are freed
up to love the other person better. With more freedom. Out of
true love, because you don't *need* something in return. You're
loving the other person because Jesus has loved you, whereas in
an idolatrous love, you love the other person because you *need*
his or her love back.

Here's a question for anyone in a relationship: If you were to
break up right now, would it feel like you're losing a boyfriend or
girlfriend, or would it feel like you're losing your god?

There's a big difference.

One will make you sad. One will make you devastated.

One you can live without. One you can't.

Obviously, if Alyssa were to suddenly pass away, I would be a
wreck. Total mess. Totally grief-stricken.

But I wouldn't be without hope.

If Alyssa were my functional savior and god, then the minute
she passed, I'd be *without* hope. And without hope, the spiral of
despair runs deep.

But I follow a God who's in the business of bringing resurrection
where there was death, beauty where there was ashes, and
streams of water in the middle of a desert. And that's why
Jesus wants us to put our identity in Him, not in relationships

or spouses—as good and as amazing as they may be. Because He is the only thing that can't be taken from us. Our job can be taken. Our house can be taken. Our spouse can die. Our boyfriend or girlfriend can break up with us. But our identity and worth that resides in Jesus can never be taken, and that means it's an unshakeable hope.

When you're in the relationship, this is why it matters so much. Because if someone is your everything, you can't truly give them what they need. Because when someone is your everything, you are too dependent on that relationship. You can only be reactionary, not proactive.

That precise feeling was the dominant theme of the first serious relationship I was ever in. And it destroyed us. When I was a freshman in college, I thought I was in love and that I was going to marry this girl. But I wasn't a follower of Jesus yet, and so I had no anchor. No true sense or center that I could give from. And it was toxic. When she wronged me or upset me or did all the myriad things that happen in a normal relationship probably every day, I couldn't help but lash out. And the same went for her. It felt like we fought every single day. I couldn't help but respond in hurt or anger because I was a slave to her since she was my everything. She was giving me my center, so when that faltered, I was undone.

But when you are getting your center from Jesus, and not from your significant other, then when they upset you or wrong you, you aren't a slave and don't have to live as a reactionary. You know that your worth and identity are coming from somewhere else, and so you can respond with grace. With love. With forgiveness. And it breaks the cycle. It lets you truly love that person.

In a deep irony, though, while our relationship was toxic—and sadly I only brought her down with me—her parents' relationship was the first I ever witnessed a godly marriage. They were incredibly solid Jesus followers. It was then, at nineteen, that I saw what having a relationship that put Jesus in the center could do. I saw how that couple communicated, how they loved their daughter, how they just bled with an example of grace, love, and humility.

How they never cut each other down.

How they lifted each other up.

How they showed love.

It was one of the most impactful experiences of my life. It's hard not to feel shame and guilt and pain over my part in that relationship, but the one saving grace was her parents. Seeing their relationship caused my wheels to start spinning in the opposite direction. That's when I became a Christian and started to walk with Jesus. That's when I had that moment of "Oh, this is what a relationship can be."

TAKEAWAY

Making your boyfriend, girlfriend, or spouse your "functional savior" instead of Jesus will always lead to despair and disillusionment. No human can carry that weight. When God is properly put on His throne to reign over our lives, we are set free to love and serve our significant others better.

04

RIDING SOLO

(Jason Derulo)

I've often heard it said that there are girls boys date, and then there are girls boys marry. Well, growing up, I fell into the "girls you marry category"—the non-flirty girls who like to have fun but are the deeper, quieter, more stable types. Which, looking back, was a good thing, but at the time, I thought it sucked. Guys, I just wanted to go on a date. Or get invited to prom. I had visions of being asked out in some creative way, like the guy organizing a scavenger hunt that leads me to a lookout over the city, where twelve dozen roses are scattered in a heart shape on the ground and where he gets down on his knee to ask me to the dance. (Okay, so I suppose that's more like a proposal, but I would have been okay with that!) But alas, there were no guys lined up to ask me out. Because I was the kind of girl you only got involved with if you were ready to get down on one knee. And that ruled out most—or all—guys.

I watched my friends in high school go to one dance after another. Start and end relationships. I heard all the stories of their first hand-hold, their first kiss, the sweet dates their guys planned. Walks at sunset. Hikes through the mountains. Bike rides on Saturdays through local markets.

It's okay, I told myself. *I'll meet someone when I go to college.* Now, I have to admit that I really didn't want to just date anyone. If I was going to get into a relationship, I wanted it to be serious. But most important, I was waiting for a guy who knocked my socks off. Someone who really loved Jesus. Not a guy who just went to church or did the youth group thing. But a guy who talked to Jesus often, who was passionate about God's glory, who read the Bible. I wanted someone to challenge me in my Christian walk, to speak spiritual truth into my life, to pray for me. Someone who would cherish me and be my best friend. I wanted to laugh often and go on adventures, and I wanted someone I could trust. Someone humble and honest.

I figured since I was going to a Christian college, I would meet my husband there. Sure, I had ambitions that would have slowed down the timeline. I wanted to study abroad, go on a long-term mission trip, graduate with honors, maybe even get my master's degree. But I also wanted my Mrs. degree!

But college came and went in three years with no ring. I had my BA but no fiancé. Not even a boyfriend. I'd had crushes on a couple of guys, but nothing ever came of it. Unfortunately, I think that guys on our Christian college campus feared for their lives because they could sense the pressure to give a girl "a ring by spring." (But guys, going to coffee does not mean the girl expects you to propose the next day! Yes, we're hoping to get married, but in a normal way. So get that girl's number. Invite her to dinner or coffee or just open her door for her.)

My first date was also my worst. It was my freshman year, and he asked if I wanted to grab dinner one night after my tennis practice. I was super excited. Right after tennis, I ran to the dorm to get ready. He came into the dorm to pick me up, and when we walked outside, he told me he walked to get me since he didn't have a car. Totally okay. I get that. I didn't have a car either.

While we walked the mile to dinner, we talked the whole way. He asked what my major was and what I wanted to do after college. At the time, I really wasn't sure what I wanted to do, but I was dreaming big, so I shared my hopes and dreams. I wanted to go overseas after I graduated. I had dreamed of being a missionary since I was fifteen. So maybe I'd teach English in Israel, or translate the Bible in Papua New Guinea. But with each dream I shared, he put it down. "That's unrealistic. They don't need that." Strike one.

When we finally got to the restaurant—ahem, Jimmy Deans—we went up to the counter to order, and he didn't order anything! He had already eaten before he picked me up. He did pay, which was very gentlemanly, but it was awkward to have him sit across from me and watch as I scarfed down a whole burger. Strike two.

Finally, on our way home, we were trying to find things that we had in common. Small things. Big things. Favorite places to visit. Favorite sports. But we had nothing in common. Not one thing. In fact, everything he liked, I hated, and vice versa.

I liked the beach; he liked the mountains.

I liked dogs; he liked cats.

I loved my sweets; he loved the salty.

I dreamed of being a Disney Princess, and he dreamed of becoming president.

Surely we could agree on food, right? I asked him what his favorite food was, and he replied "milk." *Milk?* First, who answers *milk?* Second, I was lactose intolerant! This was a total bust.

When he dropped me off at the dorm, I was just thankful it was over. Don't get me wrong: the guy was kind, and I was flattered he wanted to get to know me, but we would never have worked out. I will tell you, completely embarrassed and ashamed, that I avoided him like the plague for the next couple of months. When he came around, I hid in the bathroom. When he left messages, I didn't return his calls. I know, I know: I'm lame.

The worst part was that later, when I was totally sorry and wanted to make things right, when we saw each other on campus, he'd give me glares that could kill. I tried to say hi or wave, but he just ignored me. I felt awful, and I knew that I had so much to learn about relationships, starting with how to be kind and gracious when feelings aren't mutual.

Thankfully, later in college, I went on a few other dates that were awesome. One guy took me to a water park, and we laughed the whole day. He was literally the sweetest guy I've ever met. But when it came down to it, I just wasn't super attracted to him. Another guy pursued me for months. We e-mailed and wrote letters to each other while I studied abroad. (He was already out of college and working in the real world.) He came to visit me at Christmas and took me to Disneyland in the spring—just a short drive from where I was living at the time.

Unfortunately, I unintentionally strung him along. I liked him, as he had so many of the qualities I was looking for, but we were really different. While I totally believe in opposites attracting, our lives weren't going in the same direction. He was an ER nurse, working nights and thinking of continuing his education; I wasn't sure what I was going to do, but studying overseas was high on my list. Our lives could have come together if we had tried hard enough, but I don't think it would have been true to who we were.

The summer before I graduated, I helped lead a six-week mission trip to South Africa with a group from my college. I was a mission's major with an emphasis in teaching English as a second language. This particular trip was focused on teaching English to elementary students in a small village. Throughout the year when we met as a team to prepare for the trip, a guy named Kyle intrigued me. He was hilarious, fun, and super passionate about life. He was in the worship band, compassionate, great with kids, and we sometimes had deep conversations that made me think about life. Basically, he was my dream man in human form.

I kept my distance, however, because I thought he had a girlfriend. I wasn't 100 percent sure, but if there was any possibility of a girlfriend, I wanted to stay away. I didn't want to interfere with another relationship, and I didn't want to put my heart out on the line to someone who wasn't available.

When we finally went on our mission trip to Johannesburg, reality smacked me in the face. We had gone into the trip thinking that the two English majors on the team would be teaching two classes of English while the other teammates would help in the classroom. Well, when we got there, the teachers—who never get any vacation—gave up their classrooms. So we each ended up with our own classroom of thirty to fifty children. The kids barely spoke English, and none of them would listen to my soft, high voice. It was total chaos. On top of that, the conditions and sorrow I saw in the town were so heart-wrenching that I could barely handle it. I was freezing, hungry, and extremely homesick.

There were only nine of us on the trip, so we became close fast. And Kyle became my knight in shining armor. In the middle of hardship and heartache, he was a light. I couldn't wait to get home from school every day just to hang out with him, to have a good conversation and laugh hard. So it's no surprise that I fell hard for him. He was everything I wanted in a man. Only thing was, I still didn't know whether he had a girlfriend. But I clung to the hope that he was available.

Two weeks before the trip ended, however, Kyle started to mention his girlfriend. A lot. All of a sudden he couldn't stop talking about her. Eventually he admitted that he hadn't wanted to talk about her because our team consisted of all girls and two guys. He wanted to be considerate and focus on our mission. I was crushed. It would have been so much better if he had talked about her the whole time! *Before* my heart was totally involved. (Which, of course, he never knew.) When the trip ended, we said our goodbyes, and I never heard from him again.

The rest of the summer I was heartbroken, mostly because I couldn't imagine a more perfect guy for me, and he wasn't available. I even felt like he had led me on in a way. He was flirty at times and had seemed interested at certain points. Or that's what my brain told me anyway.

The only way I could find to heal from the loss was by praying. And a lot of running. And listening to Phil Wickham's worship music. Every day, multiple times throughout the day. That experience taught me to pray for my future husband. Whenever Kyle would come to mind, I would say a quick prayer for him, and then start praying for my husband. I had prayed for my future husband in the past here and there, but never like this. Yet it was what helped me survive. Singleness had never stung so much.

My friends were in serious relationships, and some were engaged. My best friend had just gotten married that summer. My whole life, I'd always had a plan. I would work hard in high school, get a job, go to college in California, travel, and then get married. And that was it. I had never thought past getting married. Or thought about what to do if I didn't get married. But here I was, one semester left of college, and not even a boyfriend.

Hopelessness was so tangible. But when I prayed for my future husband, I had hope. It felt as though the Spirit was leading me to pray for him at that exact moment. For the first time, I wasn't just praying for his future qualities and our lives together; I was praying for his everyday circumstances, his character, and his heart. I knew God was at work in his life in a powerful way that summer. I knew my prayers weren't just words or a fleeting hope. Rather, they were real and being heard, and God was up to something good.

The beauty of that summer was that for the first time I realized what it meant to wait on the Lord. And, oh man, I felt the wait. The longing. The desire unfulfilled. You know the feeling? Sometimes you feel like you just can't wait one more second. It's as if you're holding your breath and you're afraid that if your future husband doesn't come that exact minute, you'll suffocate. I was waiting for God to bring him into my life and to answer my prayers of so many years. But as I waited, I was actually doing *something*. I wasn't just sitting, twiddling my thumbs; I was actively waiting. On the outside it may have looked otherwise, but in my heart, I was putting action to my hope, to my ache, to my deep longing.

Prayer can be a funny thing. A deceiving thing, even, because it takes faith. It may seem like it's pointless, or like God doesn't hear us, when we don't receive immediate answers. It takes a lot of patience, perseverance, and hope. But I can assure you: God hears the prayer of the righteous.

So often we want to do things in our own strength, to take matters into our own hands, because we don't see God working. *I've waited long enough*, you may think. *I'm gonna do something.* You don't *see* anything happening, so you take the reins into your own hands and decide to pursue a guy instead of letting him pursue you. Once you're in a relationship, I totally believe you need to be pursuing him as well, but until you are, let the guy go after you.

If a guy really is interested, he'll chase you. But if he's not, he won't. It's like in the movie *He's Just Not That Into You*. I love that movie because it really is so true. If a guy likes you, he will move heaven and earth to win your heart. But if he's *not that into you*, he won't. He'll be wishy-washy and noncommittal and leave you guessing and confused. I'm not saying to sit in a corner and wait for him to come find you. Because, let's be honest, that's most likely not going to happen. You *can* put yourself out there.

Make yourself known as Ruth did when she gleaned in Boaz's garden and then went to him in the night asking him to be her kinsman redeemer. (Which totally gets lost on our generation, because women don't ask men to be their kinsman redeemers!) But you can follow her example by being available and making yourself known. Go to his soccer game. Make him blueberry muffins for his exam. If he works at a restaurant, eat there one night with your girlfriend. If he asks for your number, give it to him. If he asks you to go on a date, say yes!

There's a big difference, however, between making yourself known and available, and flat-out pursuing a guy. Sending him texts throughout the day, snapchatting, and always being the one to call him. Asking him to hang out, to come over, to grab a bite to eat. All the while, having your heart fall more and more for him, and he's just along for the ride. He enjoys the companionship, but as soon as another girl comes along who catches his eye, he'll go after her. And then you're left hurt and confused.

Other times taking matters into our own hands means we settle. There is a guy knocking on your door, but you're not totally into him. You may think you like him, but maybe you just admire him. On paper he's everything you want, but he doesn't give you butterflies. (Not that it's *all* about the butterflies! But at some point, he should make you a bit weak at the knees. Sometimes that takes a lot longer to transpire, but if it never does, then most likely he should just be in the friend zone.)

Or maybe he's not the best for you. He may be a nice guy and have a good job. You're flattered by his pursuit of you, but your friends and family are concerned. They aren't big fans and see some red flags. In your heart, you see the red flags, too, but you're willing to turn a blind eye to them because, well, you've waited long enough. Or because he's so stinkin' hot and you're just straight-up blinded by his looks and the way he makes you feel and you just can't wait one more day. Here's a guy who's here and he likes you, so you're going for it.

It's a scary thing to take matters into your own hands. Wanting to be the ruler of your life, instead of letting God. It's what Eve did all the way back in the garden. She didn't believe God. She doubted His goodness to her. His promise to her. She believed the lie that Satan laid before her, and she took matters into her own hands, and sin entered the world:

Shame.

Fear.

Disobedience.

Hatred.

Waiting is hard. I waited until I was twenty-two to date, and then twenty-five to get married, and it was so hard. But I have some really close friends who have waited much longer than I did. However long your wait is, think of it as an opportunity to trust God. Waiting is an opportunity to grow our faith. To believe in the promises that God has so graciously given us. It's not like we just sit and watch TV until the Lord does something, but rather, waiting puts us into a battle over our minds and hearts.

Do you believe that God *loves* you? That He is *for* you? That He is in *control*? That He is *all-powerful* and *able* to do anything?[1] That He is pursuing you with His goodness and mercy every moment of your life?[2] That He knows your heart, your desires, and hears your prayers?

WAITING IS AN OPPORTUNITY TO GROW OUR FAITH.

Sometimes seasons of singleness can be a breeze (and you're rocking Beyoncé's "Single Ladies" song!). You're doing great! You're loving life. Loving what you're doing, the friends you're spending time with. You are so full of hope and life. And other times, it's like you just can't go one more minute. You've waited long enough. ("Yes, ma'am. I'm *still* single. Thanks for asking.") It's a dry and desert land. Regardless of the season, God is calling you to trust Him. To enter into a deeper knowing of Him.

I participated in a conference in Oahu for girls of all ages. It was such an honor to get up on stage and speak with Jeff and then to be able to sit in the stands and listen to the other speakers. Lauren Daigle was the worship leader for the weekend. I met her and her mom backstage, and immediately had a friend crush on her. She's like the coolest girl I've ever met, and if we lived in the same town, I'd totally want her to be my best friend.

Lauren was doing a Q&A with a few of the other women speakers at the conference, and the most frequent question the audience asked was how she "deals" with being single in her early twenties. She shared how she comes from a town where everyone has their weddings planned by the age of sixteen and often literally get married the day after high school graduation. All her friends were married, and when she moved to Nashville, she made new single friends, who are all now getting married as well.

I can imagine that traveling a lot and being a professional singer makes it hard to date or find someone who really wants to be with you and not because of your celebrity status. She shared how this season of being single is an opportunity for her to enter into the presence of the Lord in a way that is so beautiful and intimate. It's just her and Jesus. She gets to spend time pursuing the Lord's heart and knowing him deeper and letting him speak to her. As she shared this, my heart pounded and my mouth dropped open a little. *Yes!*

Unfortunately, in our Christian culture, I feel like we elevate marriage to a point of idolatry. It's like you have to get married to be a varsity Christian. You're not there yet if you're still single. Everyone expects it.

There is a season for everything. And the single season, however long it may last, is a beautiful season. There are highs and lows, pros and cons, just as there are in marriage. I do believe that if you've wanted to get married and are still single, there is a time to grieve. Not that you grieve without hope, but you can grieve the loss of a dream or of the timeline you've had in your head. God knows your heart and your deep desire, and it is a good, God-given desire. If it hasn't been fulfilled yet, at least not on this side of heaven—because we'll all be married to the Lamb in eternity! He is our true Husband—you can be sorrowful and cry out to the Lord. Grieving is a good thing, a necessary thing at times.

Lauren had nailed it on the head—the single season is an incredible opportunity to run into the arms of God, to be known and to know Him in such a deep way that is a lot different from when you're married. God is calling you to get away and be with Him. And I'm not saying that once you do, once you've marked that off your list, then He'll bring your man to you. He might do that, but He might not. He wants to set you apart and be your God and call you into deeper waters. That's the joy. That's the gift for all of us—single, married, divorced, or widowed. We have Jesus. There is no greater gift. No greater treasure. Jesus alone satisfies.

My husband, as wonderful as he is, does not complete me or fill my heart. I enjoy him, and I love doing life with him, but ultimately the Lord is the one who satisfies every part of my soul. The Lord fills me with joy. The Lord knows my every thought and word and movement. He alone is the Lover of my soul. And at the end of the day, whatever happens or wherever your heart may be, you can rest knowing that you are deeply loved, cherished, and wanted by the King of kings. He knows all of you, every part, and loves you more than you will ever fathom, more than you can ever comprehend and more than anyone else ever will.

As you wait on Him, you can have His hope be the anchor of your soul. The hope that He is with you, He wants you, He desires you, He is for you, and He is working on your behalf. The hope that He hears you, He is in control, and He is good. I cling to Psalm 84:11: "The LORD our God is a sun and shield; the LORD gives grace and glory. *No good thing does the LORD withhold from those who walk uprightly*" (NASB, emphasis added).

God shines on me, protects me, and showers me with His grace and presence. And He is always, every moment of every day, constantly giving me what is best. He doesn't withhold one thing that is for my good. If I don't have something in that moment, it's because it wouldn't be best for me. I have all that I need right now, and all of it—the good, the hard, the uncomfortable, the ordinary—is for my good.

Likewise, God is giving you what is best in *this* very moment. You can trust His good work in your life. God is writing a good story just for you. It's your story. It doesn't look like anyone else's story. It's unique and set apart and beautiful. Even if it doesn't *feel* beautiful or is not what you would have written, it's good, and if you let Him, He will bring you into joy that you never thought possible. People will see that joy and say, "Wow, your God is amazing!"

But let's be honest: we don't always find ourselves in that place, do we? Often we live with unmet dreams and desires—whether it's for a short season, a really long season, or the whole time we're on this side of heaven. There will be some people who want to be married but will never have that desire fulfilled in this earthly life. There is an incredible tension, specifically in the realm of singleness, that each particular person has to wrestle down to the ground like Jacob. For some, God wants to teach you that you don't need to put your life on pause until you're married—because that might never happen. You can live your life *now*. God has hopes and dreams and plans for you as a single person, not just as a married person. Marriage isn't the finish line; Jesus is.

Yet, there is also the reality that God has given us particular desires and those can remain unfulfilled and unmet. The kingdom is coming, but it's not fully realized yet. There will still be thorns and thistles and dry ground where we were hoping for a beautiful garden. But the truth is, God told His people in the Old Testament that He would make streams in the desert. He didn't say He'd take His people out of the desert. He didn't say He wouldn't give them streams. He said He would give them those streams—water, life, breath, joy, and fullness—*in the middle of the desert.*

While God might not take us out of the desert, He will meet us there with His unfailing love and faithful character. God will be with us, and give us everything we need in that moment. He is our hope, our peace, our strength. And when we focus on that and push into that truth and that wrestle, we are where He wants us.

I know some are still longing though. Still waiting. As you hope in God, as you fight to believe His promises, you can pray. Run to God with everything. Roll your every burden to the Lord. Tell Him your ache. Your pain. Your longing. Your hopes and dreams. Your deep desires. Cry out to Him. Give thanks to Him. Lift your potential husband up to Him. Ask Him to make you into the person that He wants you to be. Pray for your future spouse. Pray faithfully. Pray for their heart, their character, their mind, their hopes, for healing and wholeness. You get the opportunity to join God in the work that He's doing in their life! It's not in vain.

My mentor told me that this waiting period, whatever you may be waiting for, is so small in comparison to eternity. It's as though you have a whole ball of yarn, and there's a five-inch piece pulled out. That piece is your waiting time right now, and the rest of the ball is eternity. This waiting is extremely small in the long view of things. I know it sure doesn't feel like it now, but it is. Whether you get married or not, whether your desires are answered on this side of heaven or not, the waiting will be over so soon. Take heart.

And while you're waiting and hoping and trusting God with your dreams, live your life. Enter into the story that God's writing for you. Don't sit back and let it pass you by because this isn't what you signed up for. Jump in, and ask God to do more than you could have ever imagined.[3] Go places. See things. Check off items on your bucket list.

Make a bucket list.

If you don't know what would be on that list, ask the Lord to search your heart. To help you dream big dreams and go on the adventures He wants you to go on. What do you like to do? What are you passionate about? What have you always wanted to accomplish? What would you regret not having done?

Do you want to travel the world? Start a blog? Own a business? Get a dog? See that band in concert? Start a study with friends? Learn to cook? Learn to build furniture? Live in a certain town? Become a foster parent? Graduate from college? Get your master's? Go to Magnolia Market? Go do it! Now is the time!

Save up the money. Find someone to mentor you in that skill. Ask older and wiser people how to start a business. Join that class. Apply to that school. Pack up your bags and move there. Don't let your life slip by just because you're waiting for the next thing. Go and do the things that God has placed on your heart. He will be with you; you won't be alone.

I'm so thankful for all I was able to do while I was single. I am a natural dreamer and have always had a bucket list, and it was the coolest thing to see how the Lord made so many of those dreams come true. I got to travel through Europe, study in Israel, ride a camel, swim with dolphins, serve in an orphanage, graduate from college, lead a girls' Bible study, hike through Yosemite, ride a jeep in Hawaii, play a sport in college (which I was terrible at, but hey, I got to play!), and learn to bake apple pie. And I am so thankful for all of it. Even in the longing and the ache, the Lord blessed me with such sweet memories and experiences. Some helped form me into the woman I am today, and others were sweet ways that the Lord showed me that He knew me and gave me the desires of my heart.

So take heart. This waiting is not in vain. There is so much hope as you wait, and you can fully open yourself up to that hope. Don't fear being disappointed. Don't fear being embarrassed or shamed. The Lord your God goes before you, and He is in your midst.[4]

TAKEAWAY

God is not done writing your story, and it's a good one. Whatever happens or wherever our hearts may be, we can rest knowing that we are deeply loved, cherished, and wanted by the King of kings.

05

FAKE LOVE

(Drake)

When I was thirteen years old, I was riding my bike around the neighborhood when I saw in an alley some pieces of paper that caught my eye. I stopped my bike and bent down to pick up what turned out to be a magazine. As I took a closer look, I had my first view of one of the most destructive things in the world—porn.

And you know thirteen is actually incredibly late now, right? As the availability keeps growing, the average age of first exposure keeps declining. The most conservative estimates say kids first see porn around eleven, and many sources are claiming it's as young as eight today. Kids are more likely to first see porn before they have even lost all their baby teeth.

For me, it wasn't long before I was fully consuming, watching, and seeking after it with no restraint. My addiction lasted until the middle of college. Even though the word *addiction* is accurate, I cringe to use it. When I was a teenage boy, every other teenage boy I knew watched it or talked about it regularly. It was a common topic of conversation, no different from discussing what we had for lunch that day. Which, in hindsight, this is part of addiction's power; it isn't usually called "addiction" by everyone.

When I started walking with Jesus in college, however, all of a sudden I had to confront the fact that I wasn't created for this distortion of sexuality. This was clear pretty quickly from reading the Scriptures and hearing God's vision for sexuality straight from the mouth of Jesus in the Gospels. Rewiring had to happen. Detangling had to take place. And the more I pulled back the curtain and tried to trace the distortion's origin, the more I ended up looking at that four-letter-word.

There were monsterlike qualities in me that were directly related to my use of pornography. I became incredibly selfish. Fast tempered. Had a horrible view of women that played itself out in every single relationship before Alyssa.

This is something we don't like to admit, but pornography actually changed me, just like a narcotic addiction does. It can change the brain's plasticity and completely desensitize your dopamine center. When people watch porn the amount of dopamine surges, which then desensitizes the brain to the same level of surge, which means more is needed for a bigger "hit," which is exactly why ordinary sex with a human being becomes no longer desirable or exciting.

There's also evidence that it shrinks the brain, and even recently a study done by Cambridge University discovered that the brain area that usually lights up when drug addicts are shown drug stimuli is the very same part of the brain that lights up when people who have watched porn before are shown explicit images. Meaning, the brain is being programmed (or reprogrammed) by porn.

In some ways, our generation is the porn guinea pig. We still don't fully know how much it truly affects us, because we are the first generation to have a complete access to it at any time and in almost any place. Think about it: we all carry in our pocket a little rectangular glowing screen that gives access to a limitless world.

I am part of the first generation who is native to the Internet age. In fact, I don't remember a time before the Internet. I've always had access to anything at any time; it's as easy as putting a .com at the end of it. By the time I graduated from high school, all the major ways we share personal information today, like Facebook, YouTube, and Twitter, were already on the scene. My mom once tried to explain to me what a fax machine was, and I had no idea what she was talking about. Kind of sounded like teleportation. (Doesn't making a piece of paper show up across the world sound more futuristic than archaic?)

I now make YouTube videos for a living, some that specifically deal with the topic of sexuality, so I have a unique front row seat to view how people are interacting and engaging online. Porn and technology have entered into this relationship as of late, and I don't see them divorcing anytime soon. A friend of mine who runs a large anti-sex trafficking organization said to me recently, "We are raising the most sexually *exploitive* and sexually *exploited* generation in all history. How do we think that will affect the world when they are older, running businesses, running for office, and being leaders of our next generation?"

I think of the Steubenville rape case a couple of years ago. If you're not familiar with it, it involved a few members of a high school football team who raped a sixteen-year-old girl when she passed out after drinking too much at one of their parties. A video surfaced during the trial that showed the guys a few hours before the rape, with the girl incapacitated, grabbing her, saying terrible things about her, and literally picking her up and throwing her around. Pure evil.

But two things became obvious when I looked at the case. The first was that to the guys, the girl was not another bearer of God's image but literally an object to use and abuse for their pleasure and entertainment. They subconsciously demoted her to subhuman status. A thing. Not a person.

And second, some of the teenagers' responses during the trial indicated that many didn't think it was rape or "that bad" since she didn't resist or say no or since it wasn't "violent." They apparently thought she existed for their pleasure and use. They thought if it wasn't violent, then why wasn't it totally okay for them to use a girl for whatever they wanted? They had been trained to think that way, and I wouldn't doubt that if you went into those teenagers' Internet history, porn sites would show recurring visits for years.

Porn is a cancer. It is unequivocally destructive to souls, marriages, relationships, jobs, and personal lives. In the last three to five years, research has shown that porn and technology, like our smartphones and social media, are rewiring our brains and messing with our brain chemistry. Think about that: it's not just something we choose to do, but it's doing something to us. Literally.

WE ARE
TERRIFIED OF
BEING KNOWN,
NOT REALIZING
THAT'S
EXACTLY
WHERE JOY
IS HIDING.

It's not a stretch to say we are remaking humanity in some regard, and not in a good way. We are fundamentally rewiring the human race. And the biggest hit we are taking—not only with porn or technology but also in how they interact with each other—is the death of intimacy.

This is why porn is so destructive. It's the very antithesis to intimacy. It inherently kills any ability for true love and intimacy—what we were created for. True, life-giving intimacy. Vulnerability. Nakedness. Being fully known and fully loved at the same time. And porn by its very nature cannot give that.

Intimacy is based on trust. True intimacy involves an exchange. Someone offers vulnerability, and the other honors that vulnerability. Then the other person reciprocates that vulnerability, creating a beautiful cycle. And that bond is exclusive and hidden; it's only for the two people to behold and be a part of. But it's the very antithesis of intimacy when one person in the relationship is secretly inviting others into that space through porn. Hundreds, if not thousands, of women's faces and naked bodies are brought into the bedroom with the husband and wife.

And because intimacy inherently needs vulnerability, porn by its nature cannot give that. It's one person, not two. And it's a computer screen, not another human being. It's getting the release of dopamine without vulnerability. You can't be vulnerable—and thus can't experience intimacy—because there's no one else there. It's hiding and short-circuiting God's true design for sex.

Few people know what it means to be intimate anymore and not just in our sexuality but platonically speaking as well. It's why whenever I'm out with friends and there's an awkward silence, we pull out our phones. We look down. We don't understand what it means to be known. In fact, I think we are terrified of being known, not realizing that's exactly where joy is hiding.

It's why we bounce around different friend groups. The minute someone might get close enough to begin to know the true us, we move on. It's why we play out most of our problems on social media—because it's the perfect platform to put our best foot forward while never having to share the hard stuff.

We have a long road in front of us, and this issue is multifaceted and complex, but one thing that would serve us well is getting to the root of the issue: objectification.

•

I think *everyone* is objectified in our culture. It's one of the symptoms of sin. But I think women endure a worse and more intense version of objectification.

Our culture teaches us that women are commodities. Objects. But they are not slaves to the male gaze. The problem with porn is it has completely commoditized sex. Sex is no longer something sacred; it's simply a consumer good. We've made an orgasm something you can buy online, usually at women's expense.

Sadly, objectification of women happens in many different spheres of the Christian world too. For example, when I'm combating porn or trafficking or lust, some of the most common things I hear people say are, *Don't look at that. Don't you realize that's someone's daughter? That's someone's wife? That's someone's sister?*

The problem is, that's tethering a woman's identity and worth and value to her relationship to a man. It's saying she only means something because of who she is related to. But the truth is, a woman isn't valued because she's someone's *daughter*; she's valued because she's *someone*. Nothing can bring more dignity than realization of a person's humanness. The sacredness of skin and bone and air and lungs and life. There's glory there. Residue of the very breath of God, breathed into us from the beginning of time, meaning any assault on us is by its nature an assault on our Creator, since we bear His image. Let's never forget that. And restoring that can help kill the objectification culture. By the way, the cousin to this is a pastor always talking about his "smoking hot wife." No. Please stop.

Sometimes it's incredibly subtle. I have a two-year-old daughter named Kinsley and a six-month-old son, Kannon. Before we had Kannon and it was just Kinsley, people would say the strangest things. Sometimes when people would see me as a dad with a daughter, they would joke and say, "Sorry" or "Congrats, but I bet you can't wait until you have a boy." As if somehow a girl is JV. Just a stepping-stone to something greater. I mean, what does that even mean? It's as if they are saying that the peak of procreation and the glory of a father is having a little human with a penis. (And yes, I just said the *P* word. Surprised me too.)

And frankly, even in the Christian world, when it comes to our best deterrents or paths to healing, we still don't realize we are implicitly doing the same thing.

I read a statement online that said "success happens when a guy looks away from porn not because of shame, but when they have such a high view of women that it's nearly impossible to get arousal from their exploitation." We need to replace the no with a better yes. The only way to create lasting behavioral change is to provide a superior pleasure.

It's like a desert. If I'm in a desert and a toilet bowl magically shows up, I'd drink that water, and I'd love it. Might make me sick the next day, but I would. But if I'm back home in Washington, where I was raised, and I'm thirsty, I don't go to the toilet. I go to the kitchen. And when I'm walking by the bathroom to the kitchen, I don't have to white-knuckle it: *Don't drink, don't drink, don't drink.* The superior option suppresses my attraction for the toilet water.

Might we be people who not only say, "Hey, that's going to hurt you, and that's not a good option" but also say, "This is better. Come this way. Come find life. Come find beauty. Come find wholeness. Come find intimacy. Come find vitality. Come find mystery."

I believe Jesus was the true human one, the prototype of new creation, and if we truly want to know what it means to be human, too, we follow Him. He never raised a hand to a woman. He never was aggressive or coercive or objectifying toward a woman. In fact, the way Jesus interacted with women was downright scandalous because of how He treated them. At that time in the first century, women couldn't even testify in court, because they weren't considered credible enough. But guess who Jesus decided to reveal His resurrection to? His resurrection—the most earth-shattering moment in all human history? Yeah, that's right—He revealed it to women.

And according to John, guess who Jesus chose as the very first person to tell that He was the Messiah, the Promised One they'd been hoping for, for hundreds of years? Yeah, a woman—a

Samaritan woman, at that, belonging to an ethnic group that during that time was seen by the Jews as half-breeds, lower class, and distorters of the truth.

And guess who the Gospels record and put into good light as the only ones who didn't abandon Jesus during His arrest and crucifixion? *Women.*

Because progress won't be made until we not only say no but also say yes. Progress won't be made until people understand that porn can't deliver what we're created for. It can't teach us that giving is better than taking, vulnerability is better than hiding, and covenant is better than contract.

But I know there will be many people reading this who may be addicted to porn or are in a place where it's crippling their relationships. What do you do then? Is there hope? Yes, there is. I experienced it.

●

I was nineteen when I first understood just how amazing Jesus is. I experienced freedom and grace and a love I will never forget. In that moment everything clicked, and I realized just how deeply the powerful Creator of the universe knew me and loved me. Immediately many things changed in me. The anger that had consumed me was gone. My temptation to shoplift and steal everything in sight disappeared. I even returned things I'd stolen, with letters of apology.

But addiction to porn? Yeah, that one didn't go away immediately. It felt like quicksand, which created a season of depression in me. I knew how destructive it was, yet I couldn't seem to stop or say no.

I think many people don't find freedom from porn because they don't treat it like the addiction it is. When people are addicted to cocaine, or alcohol, or prescription drugs, we don't just tell them to try harder. We don't tell them to *just* pray more (though yes, that's helpful). To *just* have more faith. We realize there are brain chemistry factors at work, as well as deeply ingrained biological and neurological processes, and withdrawals will happen. And so it is with porn.

If you're addicted to porn, as I used to be, please find help. Bring it into the light. Seek guidance and community and grace. What if being exposed isn't the worst thing that could happen? What if being in the dark is?

I think of a close friend, whose husband was emotionally abusive, which ended the marriage, and porn was a huge part of it.

When they were married, she sensed another woman. She wasn't certain, but she felt her presence. Whenever the marriage had a hard moment—big or small—he seemed to turn to *this other woman,* not to his wife.

A cycle was created in which she'd confront him about her intuitions, he'd deny it, and she was left with the difficult choice of believing him despite what she felt or proving him a liar. And one of the more poignant parts of her story is how she felt that the reason it was so tough and hurtful was that he had known the other girl—the one on a computer screen—longer. They had more history. More background. More years of connection and brain chemistry distortion. And the girl on the screen was hard to compete with—she didn't nag him about household responsibilities, she didn't need to be pursued, she never asked him for anything. But that's because *she wasn't real.*

Sadly, our friend's story isn't all that uncommon. We have friends whose marriages have been completely healed and put back together after the insidiousness of porn almost killed them, and we have friends whose marriages were completely destroyed by porn.

My favorite thing about the story above is our friend's wisdom in helping other couples and young women walk through the issue. One of the things she tells them is, "When it came to marriage, we just glossed over the topic and said our vows. I don't remember even thinking about having the conversation."

Sin lives in the darkness. It can't survive in the light.

So the best thing is to bring it all up. Talk about it. Ask the really hard questions. And the hardest part—be specific. Because it's through specificity that you can gain a really good idea of how serious this issue is and how pervasive it will be in a marriage. And that's something our friend is adamant about in her story. "If I could go back in time, this is the conversation I would like to have been brave enough to have."

When was the last time you looked at porn?

What was your longest binge (season of looking at it regularly)?

How long have you been sober (not looked at porn)?

How young were you when you started?

What kind of stuff are we talking about? How deep did it go?

Can I be honest? If you're dating and the history of porn is still an ongoing struggle in the relationship, please break up. Sadly, I hear over and over again that many women can't break up with their boyfriends because that's not what Jesus would do. They say, "*What about grace?*"

But you're not Jesus. And trying to be Jesus for someone else (in that you're trying to heal someone else) will crush you—and them.

Grace is God's unmerited favor toward us, and by that definition I think the most gracious thing someone can do is end the relationship so the person can get help. Heal. Walk the long and slow and arduous path of redemption, moment by moment, under the weight of grace. Staying in the relationship just muddies the waters, destroys the foundation of trust needed for a healthy future relationship, and most of the time creates an intimacy dependency. Be their friend, be kind, be compassionate, but those things have zero bearing on needing to stay in a romantic relationship in pursuit of a future marriage.

No one stays with someone when they are addicted to cocaine. You break up with them *because you love them and they need help.*

It's the same with porn. It's too blurry to be in a relationship while one person is still struggling to find freedom.

And if you're married, get help. Pursue healing and reconciliation in your marriage with full force. Repent. Get help. Do whatever it takes. Quit your job and move across the country if you have to. Call on Jesus. Lean on Jesus.

If you're reading this, and you're on the other side—the person who feels that pull and that draw to the computer screen or your phone in the dark hours of the night—let me tell you, you are so loved. I mean, like "crazy ferociously pursued and loved by the Creator of the universe" love.

And guess when He loves you the most? In the very *act* of the sin, not after. Jesus is right there, sitting in the chair next to you— broken, yet with eyes full of piercing tenderness. Calling you to something great. Calling you to something better. Waiting for the moment when you say, *"I can't do it. I'm done. No more!"*

We serve a God of resurrection. Of miracles. Of breathing life into death. And He can do that for you.

In your story.

In your past.

In your future marriage.

In your marriage now.

TAKEAWAY

Porn has reached pandemic levels in our society. Without question, it affects almost every relationship at some level. Do whatever it takes to find healing and freedom. Jesus stepped out of the grave. And because of Him, we can too.

06

LUCKY

(Jason Mraz)

I had my first "real boyfriend" at age twenty-two. I'd spent so much time waiting and longing to be married. When I was in college, I'd prayed for my future husband. I asked the Lord to make our relationship a "were it not for God" one. You know, the kind that is so evidently created by God, the couple who is so good together that only God could've written their love story because it was too good to be true, too beautiful a story to have just happened. I wanted a relationship that I could tell others was "all God." I wanted to be able to point to God's faithfulness and share how He answered all those prayers for all those years and, well, He did just that.

In the spring of 2009, I graduated from a college in Los Angeles and looked forward to a two-year internship I had lined up at a church on Maui. After I said goodbye to my roommates and friends in LA in August, I headed back home to Seattle for two weeks. I was so excited to go home for a bit after months of hardship and extreme loneliness. I was also eager to hop on a plane at the end of my visit to see what was waiting for me out there in the Pacific.

While home, I planned to attend the wedding of my friend Stacey. Her younger brother and sister, Jake and Shannon, were two of my closest friends. We'd grown up together in church and had a really close-knit youth group. We did everything together back then, and many of us were home for the wedding. I'm still close to those friends today.

A few days before the wedding, I joined my friends at the church to help set up for the reception. We stopped to buy lunch, and as we sat on the old gymnasium floor to eat burgers and fries, my friend Shannon declared, in front of our big circle of friends, "Lyss, I know someone who is smitten with you!" (Shannon grew up on old movies, has a love for older eras, and uses words like *smitten*.)

I blushed. And also was completely confused because I hadn't been home very often during the last couple of years. Who in the world would have a crush on me? Who even knew me?

All the girls asked, *"Who?"*

"Bethke!"

At first, I had no idea who she was talking about. *Bethke? Who is Bethke?* Then I remembered he was Shannon's brother's best friend. He had requested to be my friend on Facebook months before and sent me a couple of messages, but I hadn't thought much of it since I didn't actually know him. I remembered meeting him at our high school prom. He had been the guy onstage, wearing sunglasses and getting everyone pumped up to dance. He had been the center of attention. The life of the party.

All the girls started to giggle and talk about this Bethke guy. I'll admit, I was totally flattered and a bit excited. I remembered his photo. He was *cute*. And it had been so long since someone had actually liked *me*. But mostly I played it cool. I was leaving in a week for an island two thousand miles away in the middle of the Pacific Ocean. If anything, I had my heart set on meeting a surfer boy and falling in love under the Maui moon. Starting a relationship with a boy I barely knew, who was younger than me, and—as I came to find out—was leaving for college in Oregon in a week, was totally out of the question. I mean, we went to the same high school and never even hung out. Why would anything spark between us now?

I couldn't stop wondering about Jeff Bethke though. Confession: I totally stalked his Facebook profile. Isn't that what it's for? There were so many pictures of him and Jake hanging out. I gathered that he liked camping and dogs and was a leader on the baseball field. There was even a video of him sharing the gospel with eight-year-olds at a summer youth sports camp. *Okay, God, I'll be open. If you want to strike up an interaction, that'd be nice.* Not to mention he was super attractive.

On the day of the wedding, Shannon mentioned that Jeff was coming just to meet me. He hadn't been invited, but her mom said he could come if he helped clean up afterward. I wore my best dress and curled my hair. Then I waited and waited and waited for him to come up and talk to me. The wedding ceremony came and went. The reception started.

Finally, after the cake had been cut, Jeff walked over to my table, hugged me like we'd known each other for years, and started talking. I was taken aback by how familiar he seemed, how easy the conversation was, and how comfortable I felt with him. We talked as if we were best friends. Jeff shared how he had given his life to Jesus a couple of years back in college and how he'd been growing as a Christian ever since. I don't remember much more about the conversation, but I remember thinking, *There's something different about this guy.* I wanted to know more. He was so open, honest, and deep right away, and I knew he was the real deal in terms of his walk with Jesus.

That week, we ended up hanging out quite a few times with a bunch of our friends. At church. Feasting on late-night milkshakes and burgers. And at one last bonfire before we said goodbye to summer.

Jake had texted, asking if I wanted to come over for the bonfire. It was kind of a going-away party for Jeff before he left for college the next morning, but it was also my last night before I flew out to Maui. I told him I'd be over after dinner with my parents.

Little did I know that Jake and Jeff had been conspiring all week, planning different times for Jeff and me to see each other.

We all stood or sat around the bonfire, talking and laughing and roasting marshmallows. At one point, Jeff and I found ourselves sitting beside the campfire alone (sneaky friends!), and it was then that Jeff opened up more about his past. I liked how nothing was hidden with him. While he was sharing, his marshmallows caught on fire. He tried to blow out the flames, but as he did, they dropped in his lap—crotch on fire! He quickly patted his shorts down but then had gooey marshmallows all over. He was a total mess.

While Jeff left to clean up, I hung out with friends who had returned to the bonfire. When he came back, he wore a new pair of shorts and smelled of heavy cologne. *This guy is totally into me,* I thought. And I was totally interested in him.

I stayed as long as I could, knowing that if I stayed up too late when I had an early flight the next morning, I'd regret it. I just wanted Jeff to give some indication that we'd stay in touch. He still hadn't even asked for my phone number.

Finally, I stood up and told everyone I had to go.

Jeff jumped up and blurted out, "Um, so do you have a phone?"

I tried not to giggle. *Dude, it's the twenty-first century.*

"Yeah," I said coyly.

Clearing his throat, Jeff asked, "Um, can I get your number then?"

I gave him my number, hugged him, and left. I didn't know what would happen, but at least there was hope as we went our separate ways.

●

During the next couple of months, Jeff called me and we'd end up on the phone for hours. He was so easy to talk to. There was never a lull in the conversation, and what we did talk about was encouraging and soul-filling. Jeff was smart and made me think about things differently.

Then suddenly, that October, I didn't hear from him. Not once. No phone calls. No text messages. No Facebook. I totally thought he was over me. I figured it was just too hard being that far apart. I still thought about him a lot but honestly just didn't see how it'd work out anyway, so I gave up.

Then, out of the blue, that November, he called me and talked to me as if nothing were amiss. (*Hello . . . I haven't heard from you in a month!*) After a few minutes, he jumped into a spiel about how he had been listening to a sermon and the pastor was saying that when you find a girl who loves Jesus, don't let her go. Go after her. He told me he realized that he didn't want to let me go and asked if I'd be his girlfriend. He wanted to see where things could go with us and intentionally wanted to get to know me better to see if maybe marriage was in our future.

It all felt so right. I had never met anyone like Jeff before, and even though I had no idea how it would work out, I really wanted to get to know him better too. So I agreed. And so began our relationship.

We talked on the phone regularly and texted and e-mailed each other. (Yes, e-mail. It was a thing back then.) We had to be creative with how we pursued each other, being two thousand miles away. We would send each other cards and gifts. I remember making him a Thanksgiving card, a turkey made out of my thumbprint, and sending him a candygram for Valentine's Day. I made him homemade puppy chow (Chex mix covered in peanut butter, chocolate, and powdered sugar. I mean, if that doesn't win a guy's heart, I don't know what will! (Well, maybe a steak.) I sent it in a box, and I still remember him calling to thank me as he shoveled it into his mouth.

When I went home for Christmas that year, we finally got to spend time together face-to-face. It was a little awkward at first because we hadn't been together in person much more than a few days, and now all of a sudden we were together as a couple. But we spent almost every day together. We laughed and talked about everything and anything. The more I hung out with him, the more I liked him. In fact, by the end of the two weeks, I was totally in love. Head in the clouds and over the moon. I was so clumsy all the time because, honestly, I was always thinking of Jeff. My mom noticed it too. She just laughed at how crazy I was about this guy.

Throughout the rest of that school year, I saw Jeff every couple of weeks. I flew to visit him at college for a weekend, and when his baseball team came to Oahu for a tournament, I hopped islands with my friend Risa to see him. Then he came out in May to visit for two weeks. I was so excited, I couldn't contain myself! Finally, we were going to be with each other for a good chunk of time.

I had all these hopes and expectations for our time together. Though I still had to work for a church for one of the weeks Jeff was here, I figured he would come to the events with me or would hang out in the office during the day, and we would do fun things together before and after work. Ride bikes to a local breakfast spot, play tennis, read our Bibles at Starbucks (because, clearly, that's what a Christian couple does!). My parents were flying out for the other week and had rented a hotel room for all of us as a vacation.

Those two weeks with Jeff were like a roller coaster. Big highs and low lows. Well, in my heart anyway. On the surface, we were great. We played in the pool, walked the beach, gallivanted around the island. But the whole time, I felt like Jeff was holding back. Honestly, I had begun to wonder if he even liked me anymore. I was afraid that I was totally in love with this guy, that I was ready to say yes if he popped the question, but he wasn't really feeling it in return. He wasn't very affectionate, and the one time I tried to bring up the *M* word, he quickly changed the conversation, as if he was terrified.

The week that I had to work, he didn't visit me at the church one time. I had to beg him to come to youth group with me. Looking back, I think I had these dreams of us being a team and me being on mission with my boyfriend, but it didn't seem like Jeff wanted to join me. I was so torn. I loved him. He gave me butterflies all the way to my toes, and I'd never met a guy who loved Jesus the way he did. But after I dropped him off at the airport, I knew we needed to break up.

It hit me the night I was flying out with some of my youth group to go on a two-week mission trip. I had just gotten off the phone with my mom, telling her my doubts about Jeff, that he didn't seem to like me much. How would we even work? He was still in college, with one more year to go. I didn't want to leave Maui ever, and he wanted to stay in the Pacific Northwest forever. He certainly wasn't ready to commit to marriage, and I was ready to move forward.

I thought he'd want to be more a part of my life by helping out with the high schoolers at the church and seeing what I did day to day, but instead he kept his distance. As the plane took off that night, big tears dropped onto my cheeks. I knew I had to break up with him. Later that night, I put my face into my pillow and cried until I fell asleep, and I did that every night for most of that mission trip.

When I got home, there was a package waiting on the front porch with my name on it from Jeff. My heart sank a little. I brought it inside, plopped it on my bed, and opened it. There was a long handwritten note saying how much he liked me, what a great time he'd had while in Maui, and how much he missed me. Then, below the note was his favorite baseball sweatshirt. I pulled it out of the box and held it up to my nose. *Sean Jean.* Jeff had sprayed it with his cologne. He knew how much I loved his scent and would always spray his letters with his cologne. The only thing better was a sweatshirt so that when I wore it, it smelled just like him.

Sigh.

This certainly didn't make breaking up with him any easier. He had no idea what was coming.

I waited as long as I could, but finally called the next day. He knew something was up. Why else would I have waited to call him?

We talked and caught up for a couple of minutes, and then I laid it on him.

"Jeff, I have to break up with you."

"What, why?"

"I don't know why, really. I just know I need to call things off."

"But I don't understand. *Why?*"

I tried to explain myself, but I couldn't. I had doubts, but I couldn't quite wrap my mind around them. I loved him, and yet it seemed wrong. The worst part, though, was that I couldn't share any of my true thoughts or reasons with Jeff, because I didn't know how to handle conflict. How could I possibly tell him something that would hurt him? How could I tell him how I really felt? About doubts I was having? And besides, even if I did, I already had decided in my heart of hearts what to do. There was no turning back now. The worst part of all was that after two weeks of crying, I had no emotions left. I was as stoic as a statue. No emotions. No tears. Nothing.

Jeff cried. It's still the only time I've ever heard him cry. I thought, *Maybe this guy really does like me after all.*

"Well, could we just take a break? Can we see how things go?"

"No. We're done. Forever."

I was brutal.

Months passed, and they were the hardest few months of my life. I thought that since I was the one to break up, I should be strong and ready to move on. But in reality, I was just as broken. Morning after morning I would sit on my cushy, worn-out, gray couch, with my coffee in one hand and Bible and journal in my lap, as big teardrops decorated the pages.

Why, God? Why couldn't he have been the one? Why did I have to fall so hard for him? Why did I break up with him? Why wasn't it right?

That summer I fought the fears that had been building my whole life. *What if I never get married? What if I'm alone forever?*

TAKEAWAY

Sometimes relationships bring up deep fears and questions. God never deserts us. He wants us to share those fears and questions with Him.

07

CALL ME MAYBE

(Carly Rae Jepsen)

I first met Alyssa on my friend's fridge.

Odd, I know.

Let me explain.

After my freshman year of college, I reconnected with a high school friend, Jake. He was one of those rare people in high school who actually took the Lord seriously. We played baseball together and even had some classes together, so we got to know each other enough to have fun while in school. But because our lives were on different paths, we didn't really become close.

So Jake was the first person I messaged when I was down at college and had all these questions about faith, Jesus, the Bible, and so on. To this day he's one of my best friends and an honorary uncle to our kids.

But during the summer after my freshman year, we were hanging out a lot. One night I was over at his parents' house with him, and a picture on their fridge of this cute girl caught my eye. Now, mind you, they had the classic Christian fridge and bulletin board where there were about five million pictures of missionary families, senior photos, Christmas postcards, and more. So saying this one picture caught my eye is saying a lot. A true "needle in a haystack" moment.

I believe my exact words when I saw the picture were, "Wow. That girl is cute. You should let me get at her."

Which, in nineteen-year-old embarrassing language, means, "That girl is beautiful. Can you introduce us?"

I remember the family hearing that comment and pretty much laughing it off, basically saying with their eyes and body language, "Not a chance."

Little did I know, Alyssa was basically Ms. Holy McHolyson. Mr. Rogers reincarnated. Or at least, that's what it seemed, based on how everyone who knew her talked about her—*Oh, she's just the sweetest. Alyssa is the best. Kindest girl ever.* It sounded like she was born right into the baptismal and accepted Jesus as her personal Lord and Savior right there in the delivery room. All joking aside, it was clear she was an incredible girl raised by solid Christian parents. She never had a wayward season in her life, started college early, then graduated *magna cum laude.* Just straight Pleasantville in a person.

And then there was me: Messy past. Lots of baggage and issues. So I think they had trouble seeing us together.

But I was persistent. Whenever I was at their house, I'd always make a side comment, asking them to introduce me or pass the word along. (I think at this point I was already Facebook stalking her. Don't lie—you know you've done it too.)

A few months later Jake's sister was engaged and planning her wedding at their church. Her parents were doing a lot of the work themselves, so Jake's mom finally said, "Jeff, if you promise to help us clean up after, take off tablecloths, and break down tables, you can come to the wedding and meet Alyssa."

Mission "Get in the Same Room as Alyssa" was in full effect. Just call me Jason Bourne.

What I didn't know was that from that moment until the wedding, my interest in Alyssa was making its way around the church hotline. When I walked into the wedding, I remember noticing a lot of eyes looking at me. Was my zipper undone? Did I have toilet paper stuck to my shoe? It took me a while to realize that everyone was waiting and watching for me to make a move on Alyssa. And of course everyone knew this, including Alyssa, except me.

I remember spotting her the minute I walked in, but I purposely kept my distance, because, well, nerves. In fact, I'm not sure I would have ever mustered up the courage to talk to her if it hadn't been for a sly move by her dad.

After the ceremony and during the reception, I was outside getting some air. This older guy I didn't know started to talk to me. We hit it off pretty well. He was a sports guy. I was a sports guy. We lived in a fairly small town, and since the high school baseball team I played on was ranked nationally that year, he started asking me questions about that. Finally, after about twenty minutes of conversation, he said, "Hey, I'm going inside. You should come with me. I want you to meet someone."

I agreed and began walking with him toward his table. All of a sudden it clicked. He was Alyssa's dad, and I had about 0.31359 seconds to compose myself for the big moment. I think I blacked out temporarily. Meeting the girl of your dreams is already intimidating enough, but meeting her for the first time when you aren't quite ready—and in front of her dad and friends—is a whole new level of awkwardness and anxiety.

I sat down, and she and I began chatting. It was one of those rare moments when everything just starts clicking. The conversation was easy, fresh, and exciting. Surprisingly, we started to go pretty deep pretty quick, and by the end of the night, we had exchanged summaries of our life stories. But I had been caught off guard by the fact that she was about six days from leaving for Maui, where she planned to work at a church for a couple of years.

It was in that moment I had to make the split-second decision to either give up (because it isn't realistic to start a relationship with a girl who leaves in six days), or go for it (as much as I could before she left).

I chose the latter.

Thankfully, because of our mutual friends, it was really easy to hang out almost every night that week, and by the time we got to the end of the week, I was in love. This was the girl I was going to marry. Sure, that might seem fast and a little early, but for anyone who knows me, I make decisions incredibly fast. I'm not really a vacillator.

The last night before Alyssa left for Hawaii, we were at a friend's house, where a small bonfire had been specifically set up for me to have another excuse to hang out with Alyssa. So everyone pretty much knew why we were there. Awkward again.

But about halfway through the night, Alyssa and I were sitting next to each other just enjoying our conversation. I was roasting a marshmallow at the time. I wasn't really paying attention, because, well, there was the personification of beauty, poise, and grace to my right. So my multitasking game was weak that night. Then someone yelled, "Jeff, your marshmallow is on fire!"

I tried to play it cool, since I actually like my marshmallows burned (really, I do). I pulled it away from the fire slowly, as if I'm not startled at all, and right when I bring it up to my mouth to blow it out, it fell off the stick. Directly on top of my zipper. And it was still on fire. I literally had a flaming ball of marshmallow sitting on my lap.

And I was no longer convincing anyone that I was playing it cool. I stood up and started dancing around, frantically patting and swatting at my shorts.

When it was all said and done, my khaki shorts were mostly white and ashy on the front section, and our friends were dying laughing. Of course, my first thought was, *What an epic fail in front of this girl I'm trying to impress.* (Later, when I found out Alyssa thought it was cute and funny, I got over my embarrassment.)

I decided to go out to my car and put on a new pair of shorts but then realized I smelled pretty terrible. To make matters worse, I figured, like any nineteen-year-old boy, I could just cover up the charred smell with a gallon of cologne—Axe body spray, which is definitely not the bestseller at your local Macy's. (By the way, scent etiquette should be mandatory sometime in middle school. For some reason, there is a huge temptation for guys under twenty-one to completely overdo it, which is why, to this day, every time I see Axe body spray, I think of the middle-school boys locker room that basically looked like it had been the site of a fog machine party and smelled terrible.)

Not only did Alyssa almost pass out from the sheer force of cologne, but the scent didn't even smell good, because it was mixed with the smell of burned ash. Then I ended the night with probably one of the more awkward moments of my life. I knew if we were going to keep talking after she moved to Hawaii, I needed to get her number. I hadn't asked for it yet, and I knew that night was my last chance.

To make matters worse, our friends did that thing they do, where they are trying to help but making it too obvious. They (all six of them) left the backyard at the same time to give Alyssa and me a chance to hang and chat one last time. And it was in that moment I was supposed to get her number.

I chickened out.

They came back out.

Nearing midnight Alyssa said, "Okay, I think I'm going to head home . . ." with a tone that was very much *hint, hint, this is your last chance.*

And me, realizing in that moment it was do or die, I just practically yell, *"Do you have a phone?"*

Not: "This was so much fun. Can I walk you out?" and then ask.

Not: "Talk about an incredible week. Is it okay if we exchange numbers to keep in touch?"

Nope.

Do you have a phone?

Like, what kind of question is that?

Then dead silence.

She says sure, and we exchange numbers. Mission accomplished, as awkwardly as possible.

Little did I know, that night she'd fly twenty-five hundred miles to Hawaii, and we'd begin getting closer and closer and then begin dating long-distance.

I think maybe the hardest part of our relationship was that it was very much on-the-job-training. I had never been in a healthy relationship. I had never dated a girl and honored her dreams, heart, goals, and body. I had never been in a relationship that had much purpose beyond young adolescent feelings.

I didn't know what to do or how to act. Of course, I was trying, and I was asking mentors for advice, and I was piecing it together. But it's clear, looking back now, I still had to work on a lot of things. And that's the special part about God's grace—looking back, Alyssa and I know that He met us where we were and carried us through.

But at that time, I still had a lot of work to do. Alyssa being incredibly mature and taking a much different teenage and college-age path than I did, and not having experienced the years of bad choices and baggage was almost like a bright mirror showing me all the places my past had affected me.

Of course the Lord forgave me, and I had found so much healing and truly been changed by understanding grace for the first time. But there's also a tension there. I think it was the theologian D. L. Moody who said, "If you cut off your leg, God will of course forgive you. But that doesn't mean your leg is growing back."

Our lives before we get into a relationship affect us deeply in the relationship. But at the same time, I was super excited to be able to connect with Alyssa. And so full of joy. Because I could tell this felt different. I could tell doing it the right way, *was the right way.* I could tell asking mentors for advice, and then them pressing me on certain things, was one of the greatest gifts I could've asked for while Alyssa and I were dating. Trying to have a healthy relationship without older, seasoned mentors is like trying to climb Mount Everest without gear and water. You can try, but it won't end well.

TAKEAWAY

We need to do relationships the right way—not just because it's the "right" thing to do but because it leads to more life, joy, and vitality. Simply put, it saves everyone a lot of heartache. True joy is at stake, and remembering that makes all the difference.

TRYING TO HAVE A HEALTHY RELATIONSHIP WITHOUT OLDER, SEASONED MENTORS IS LIKE TRYING TO CLIMB MOUNT EVEREST WITHOUT GEAR AND WATER. YOU CAN TRY, BUT IT WON'T END WELL.

08

BLEEDING LOVE

(Leona Lewis)

In the early fall, during the time that Jeff and I were broken up, a guy from church started pursuing me. I wasn't ready to date again, but this guy wouldn't give up. He was so thoughtful and I was flattered. He would bring me Starbucks when I was working in the bookstore and pick me up in the morning for a quick paddleboard session before going into the office. He took me to dinner often and brought me soup when I was sick in bed. I honestly didn't know if I was really into him, but he was sweet and handsome, and I'd never been pursued like that before. Within a month we were officially dating. I had some doubts but tried to shake them off, telling myself it couldn't hurt to just get to know someone better while dating.

A couple of weeks after we started dating, Jeff texted me out of the blue, "Hey, Alyssa. Can we Skype this week?" I thought it was so random. I mean, we had texted and e-mailed friendly messages a bit here and there since breaking up, but nothing more. I was curious about what he wanted to talk about, so I agreed.

One day, after having just gotten home from work, I heard *bloop, bloop, bloop.* (Skype sounds!) My heart skipped a beat when I saw Jeff on the screen. Man, he looked good after all these months.

Immediately, Jeff jumped into a long speech. He told me that since breaking up, he'd really grown. He realized that he had still been healing from his former relationship, which had made him scared to open up again and take risks. He wanted to be a man and take a risk with his heart again. He told me that he loved me and that he wanted to marry me, not today, but one day. He'd even move to Maui if that meant being with me. He went on and on. He told me everything I had yearned to hear for so long. *He loved me. He'd do whatever it took to be with me.* But it was too late. Finally, he asked, "So, Lyss, what do you think?"

"Jeff, thank you. I've wanted to hear those things for so long, and I'm so glad you're growing and the Lord's been showing you things. But Jeff, I'm already dating someone else. His name is Chad."

●

Chad and I had been dating for about three months when he took me on a special picnic dinner to celebrate Valentine's Day together. We went to a beach down the road that had a big grassy hill and a barbeque. He laid out a blanket, put salmon on the grill, and got the rest of the dinner ready as we watched the sunset. Everything was so dreamy. He gave me a vase full of a dozen red roses and handed me a little note all rolled up like a secret message. I opened it, and as I began reading it, tears came to my eyes. He poured out his heart to me, and then at the end told me that he loved me. How romantic! I looked at him,

smiled, and he repeated the words to me, "Alyssa, I love you.
Really. I love you."

I had never heard those words in person from a guy before. They
quickly clung to my heart and made a home there. I had had a lot
of doubts up to this point while dating Chad. I just wasn't sure
if he was the guy I was supposed to be with, but these words
sealed it for me, and that night my heart shifted. I could see us
together. Maybe I loved him too.

Then, three weeks later, late at night, he drove over to my
apartment and broke up with me. Just like that. It was totally
unexpected. I was shocked. I mean, the guy had been telling me
for months how he wanted to marry me and that marriage was the
goal we were going after. He never had any doubts or complaints.
He was always so solid and convinced of our relationship. But he
ended it. Right then and there. And never looked back.

He didn't want me. Rejection rooted deep into my heart. Lies took
hold. I was too emotional. I wasn't worth fighting for or keeping.

He didn't say any of those things to me in so many words, but it's
amazing how our hearts can take words and twist them to believe
lies. It was as if Satan were whispering them into my ear, and as
soon as I took hold of them, they became shouts that I had to live
with for years.

Soon after Chad broke up with me, Jeff reentered the scene.
He sent me a brief message, asking how I was doing. Although
it was nice to hear from him, at the time I was so over guys that
I didn't want anything to do with him. Slowly my heart softened,
however, and I became open to starting a friendship with Jeff

again. We messaged back and forth throughout the rest of
the semester, offering forgiveness and restoring our broken
relationship.

I had been so cold with Jeff—I had broken up with him suddenly
without any explanations. Chad breaking up with me was painful,
but it was also humbling. I realized that he had broken up with me
essentially the same way I had broken up with Jeff. And for the first
time, I started to understand how much I had hurt Jeff. As we talked,
Jeff was nothing but kind, humble, and gracious. I opened up a little
about my breakup with Chad, and he was compassionate.

As that next summer unfolded, I was still in Maui on my internship,
and Jeff was looking for a job now that he had graduated from
college. As our texts, calls, and messages continued, my heart
slowly healed and grew to love Jeff again. For so long I had
thought that true love was bringing your girlfriend her favorite
coffee drink at work, which is great, but really it's always having
hope, trust, perseverance, and protection.[1] And that's exactly what
Jeff did. He never stopped loving me. He waited for me, hoped
for the best, hoped for a renewed relationship, and hoped for the
best in my character. He never spoke ill of me but protected me.
He was first a friend who genuinely loved and cared for me, and I
felt humbled and in awe of him because of that.

When we saw each other in person, our reunion was full of hope
and doubt and crazy. I was in Portland for a few days, and we'd
planned to meet up. I was a nervous wreck before we met. Who
knew what would happen? I mean, we were friends now, and I
was kind of liking him, but I had no idea where he stood. I didn't
know if he had a girlfriend or was pursuing someone else. We
met up at our favorite bookstore, where we talked and laughed.

And then it ended. He had to go back to school, and I needed to fly back to Maui. I cried the whole way to the airport. My poor mom! I'd expected that he'd bring up us at some point. You know, have some type of DTR (define the relationship) talk. But no, he'd just kept it casual.

That night when I got home, we texted back and forth until early into the morning. We were finally totally honest with each other. Jeff mentioned that he did like me but was scared. I admitted the same thing. We didn't promise each other anything, but at least we knew where we stood and were continuing our friendship.

In July I flew home for a visit, and while there, I admitted to myself how crazy I was for Jeff. The more we'd talked during the last four months, the more I liked him. We squeezed in as much time together as possible—tennis, frozen yogurt, late-night chats, and cuddles. I remember being crazy for him yet also being fearful to retry our relationship. What if it failed *again*? He didn't come out so boldly as to ask me to be his girlfriend, but he hinted at it. I just poured out my doubts and fears to him and flew back to Maui.

As I was telling my friends about my time with him, Leslie asked, "So you know you like him and that you want to date him eventually, but you don't want to right now? Why not? What are you waiting for?"

That night I also talked with my mentor, and she could tell I was already in love with Jeff. But I had so many fears and was afraid to risk again. Afraid of getting hurt once more. She told me that my heart was the Lord's, so I didn't have to protect myself. He'd protect me. I could risk because my God was my Protector.

She then went on to say, "Alyssa, you know how when you guys had that Skype call long ago and Jeff got so angry that you were dating Chad? He said no one could love you like he could? Well, girl, he was *fighting* for you. He didn't want to give up. He didn't want to give *you* up."

It was the first time I understood what a great quality that was and how that alone showed how Jeff loved me. He wasn't willing to just let me go.

I knew Jeff was different from the first time we dated. God was working on him and healing him on a deep level. And he was risking. For me. There was no denying his intentions.

During that time I had also grown. I had put so many high expectations on Jeff before, ones he couldn't possibly meet. I wanted the relationship to be perfect, with no conflict. I wanted him to know what I needed, what I was thinking and feeling, without me having to say anything. I was learning that relationships are messy, but the important thing is how you go about it together. We needed to have open conversations, forgiveness, humility, and willingness to learn.

That same week I called Jeff and told him I really liked him and would love to date again. I would be moving back home in a month to start a new job, and I was hoping he'd be there too. I knew he was waiting for me to say those words. He had tried so many times to be with me, so I knew I was the one who had to make the next move if we were ever going to become an "item" again. Instead of ending the phone call with a new relationship status, however, I was left totally hopeless yet again.

"Lyss, I just don't know where I'll be in two months. I still haven't found a job, and I applied to five different jobs in different states. I could end up in Chicago by the end of this month, and where would that leave us? Long-distance again. I don't want to do that to you. I just don't know if we can be together. I need to see what happens."

I had put my heart on the line, and it was crushed. Tears streamed down my face as I thought it would never happen again for Jeff and me.

We continued to talk and, as the month rolled out, he ended up getting a job in our hometown. I was convinced that things were looking up. The week I moved home, Jeff was gone, at a camp where he was a counselor. But he had left an envelope waiting for me. It contained a long letter and a CD of songs that perfectly summed up the last year we were apart.

All week I played that CD in my car as I traveled back and forth from work, and I bawled like a baby. Songs of being broken up, of having a broken heart, of the hope of getting back together, of what a great girl I was. And during every song, with tears streaming down my face, I'd think, *Oh my gosh. It's true. I said that! I felt that. He felt that. That is how I felt. Jeff knows me so well!*

The day Jeff got home from camp, I drove over to his house and planted a big kiss on his lips. I had been waiting to do that for months. Jeff was shocked—and super excited. From then on, we were together.

Dating the second time around was a million times more wonderful than the first time. We talked about everything. He could read me like a book. I told him when I was hurt or upset, and we worked through conflict. I loved being around him and doing life with him. Being in community together. Doing studies together and discipling together. I was ready to marry him. Which probably was our biggest source of conflict. I was ready, but he was still unsure as to what the future held. He wanted a steadier job to make sure he could support us. I mean, he was living in a house with ten other guys, sharing a bunk bed with his best friend! He commuted an hour and a half one way every day. He knew I was the one he wanted to marry; he just wasn't in a position to commit yet.

Then Jeff started making YouTube videos and speaking, and suddenly he was traveling to more and more speaking engagements. Since I was a counselor at a Christian high school, I didn't get to see him much. He was gone more than he was at home. He quit his day job, and he surfed the wave God had given him. He was totally in his element and finally had a vision for his life. And he knew that he wanted me in it. He didn't want to keep going without me in it.

•

The other day I was cleaning out one of our drawers and came across some old pictures of when Jeff and I dated. As I looked at each one, I remembered all the feelings. The butterflies. The doubts. The "I love you. I know I love you." Dating can seem like a roller coaster. Even if it's with the one guy you know you'll be with forever. And then there are the breakups and broken hearts. Dating brings up so many fears, childhood pains, doubts, and then a crazy amount of excitement, hope, expectation, and joy. It's a wild ride. And nothing really prepares you for it.

I had been raised with the belief that I should date only someone I was considering marrying. While I think this philosophy was helpful in giving me a purpose in dating and avoiding additional hurt and pain, I took it too seriously. I was so afraid of dating someone who wasn't going to be my husband that I ran from any guy who said hi to me. I was nervous even talking to guys. I didn't want to kiss anyone until I kissed my husband at the altar, but that put a lot of pressure on my relationships.

When I finally started dating Jeff, I put so many expectations on him because *this was the guy*. Or at least I hoped so. I didn't bring up any conflict or share any hurt feelings, because I wanted our relationship to be perfect. I didn't want him to think I didn't have it all together. I didn't want to lose him or make him run because I admitted my doubts. I wanted him to talk about marriage and profess his love for me profusely, a few months into dating, which, for us, would have been premature.

If Jeff had said all those things when I had wanted him to, it would have moved our relationship too far ahead when it wasn't ready. I realize that you can say all those things, but if it's not the right timing, if it's too early in the relationship and you don't know for sure that you'll be together yet, it's just manipulation. It's leading someone on and getting their hopes up. Making sure you have a hold on them, when in fact you're not ready to fully put those words into action. Those words can't be spoken lightly. I'm so thankful Jeff waited to say those things until he knew he was going to be with me forever. He didn't use his words to lead me astray but instead to protect my heart.

For me, as someone who is prone to fear and worry, dating brought up a lot of fears. What if it didn't work out? What if he rejected me? What if I chose not to be with him? What if our friends and family didn't think this was a good idea? What if he didn't think I was good enough? What if this wasn't the Lord's will? What if the Lord didn't have a husband for me after all? Then what?

Yes, then what? God used dating in my life to draw out those fears I had and to replace them with His truth. It couldn't be done with a simple verse or Bible study. I had to go through the trials and fire to really come to believe and know His character and truth. Some of my biggest fears did come to pass. Two relationships ended in a breakup. I was rejected. I was told that I wasn't good enough.

Not all my friends and family thought my relationship with Chad was the best. I was so afraid of it being named a failure—or rather, me being a failure. I didn't want to appear weak or messy. I wanted to have it all together. I didn't want to have a relationship end, because how did I know for sure that another one would start? It's like you have to go back to square one when you go through a breakup. And the longer you date someone, the scarier that can become. I wanted to control the relationships, to make sure that everything went according to my plan. And I really didn't want to get hurt. I wanted to be loved and cherished and to honor the guys I was with. I wanted to treat them so well that their wives would thank me one day if it didn't work out between us.

I came to discover that the "then what?" was God. When those things happened, when my world came crashing down, when my heart felt like it was crushed into a million pieces, then God was still with me. He loved me more than I could know or understand. He didn't change. And His love for me didn't change. He was still the God of hope and healing. He was still the God of promises and faithfulness. He made me strong through those trials, matured me in ways that I needed, and drew me so much closer to Himself.

That realization didn't happen overnight or in one stupendous flashing moment. It happened in all the quiet, lonely moments when it was just me and God. The mornings when I would read my Bible and journal with big tears rolling down my cheek and onto the pages. The miles I would run in the hot sun, with worship music blaring in my ears and my heart crying out to the Lord. The nights I would cry myself to sleep, or in the moments I would sneak away at work to go pray in the bathroom.

In those moments, the Lord carried me. He was close. He didn't check out and let me handle it on my own. He drew closer than ever before and held me tight. He whispered to my weary heart, "I'm here. I love you. I'm not going anywhere." He let me be messy, cry, and ask the questions. And slowly, over time, He healed my heart and helped me to trust Him.

After Jeff and I broke up, I would spend every morning on my couch, Bible and journal in my lap, drenched from the tears that poured down my face. Yes, I was the one who broke up with Jeff. Because of that, I was supposed to be the strong one, right? That's the lie I believed, anyway. In reality, it's a loss no matter who breaks up with who, and we still have to grieve that relationship. I had loved Jeff, yes, but he was also a good friend who I chose to say goodbye to, and that was hard. I also grieved for what could have been, what I had hoped for. But the Lord showed me that regardless of who comes and goes in my life, He will always be with me, and He is enough. He alone satisfies my soul.

Then, after Chad broke up with me, I also had a lot of hurt I had to heal from—lies that I believed about myself that stung and stuck for a long time. For the first time in my life, I had to forgive someone, even when they didn't ask for forgiveness. I held on to my anger for a long time. *How could he?* He had made promises he couldn't follow through on. He blindsided me. I had to come to a place where I forgave him and then moved on.

I hate the phrase "forgive and forget" because it's impossible. You can't just forget the hurt that's been done to you. It affects your life and hits you deeply. And in relationships, this is especially true. When you choose to forgive someone, however, it's not a one-time thing. It's an ongoing action. You forgive in that instance, and then whenever it comes to mind again, you remember you forgave that person and choose not to dwell on the sin committed against you.

In the Old Testament, there are countless times when the people of Israel built an altar, like a stack of rocks, to commemorate an event. Maybe it was that God led them through the wilderness, or parted the river, or did something miraculous, and they wanted to remember who God was in that moment. So they gathered rocks and made a memorial, and whenever they walked by it, or when their great-grandchildren passed it one day, they'd be reminded of God's faithfulness and steadfast love.

When we forgive someone, it's as though we're building an altar in that moment to mark it with grace. It's done. We forgave them, and although it takes time to heal, we no longer have bitterness or anger, but rather are choosing grace. I had to build my altar of forgiveness with Chad and move on. I didn't want to be consumed with anger or resentment any longer.

Funny thing is, although he didn't break up with me in the best way, it actually was the most loving thing to do. I'm so thankful he called things off the moment he knew our relationship wasn't forever. I found out later that his mentor had told him that if he knew he wasn't my Prince Charming, he needed to get off the horse so my real Prince Charming could come along. Even though it stung like ripping off a Band-Aid, I'm so glad he did. He didn't waste my time. He didn't lead me on any further. And although I was so hurt that he didn't talk to me afterward, it really did help me to move on. He gave me space. He knew my heart was still attached, and if he had continued to call and text and try to see me, it would have made my healing process that much harder and longer.

There are so many different reasons to break up. And no matter what, you're not going to do it perfectly. It will hurt. But sometimes the most loving thing to do is to break up. If you know they're not the person you want to spend the rest of your life with, then break ties. If there are red flags, then break up. While there weren't any red flags in either of my relationships, sometimes it just isn't the right timing or the right person. Red flags, however, are important to pay attention to. If the person you're seeing is controlling in any way, manipulative, has a wandering eye, has anger issues, drinking issues, is addicted to porn, or friends and family don't think he or she is the best, you need to call it off.

Unfortunately, a lot of people may see these warnings and disregard them because they have been with the person for too long or are afraid of what may or may not happen. They decide to settle, thinking there is no one else out there or they've waited too long. Or they simply may be so infatuated with the person they're dating that they are blinded. But, y'all, as someone who is on the

IF THE PERSON YOU'RE SEEING IS CONTROLLING IN ANY WAY, MANIPULATIVE, HAS A WANDERING EYE, HAS ANGER ISSUES, DRINKING ISSUES, IS ADDICTED TO PORN, OR FRIENDS AND FAMILY DON'T THINK HE OR SHE IS THE BEST, YOU NEED TO CALL IT OFF.

other side of dating and who has friends who have been married for a while now, that stuff just follows into your marriage and gets worse. It will wreak havoc on a marriage. On you. On your heart. It is so much better to break ties now than to enter into a covenant with someone and be in bondage over those things. For both of you.

I've learned that there can be beauty in any relationship. When we are choosing Jesus and following Him, *nothing is in vain*. Any relationship you are in, any breakup you go through, is not in vain. It wasn't a failure. God, in His might and goodness, can use it to mature you and make you more whole and holy. It can teach you what things are important in a relationship and how to relate to the opposite sex. It can give you communication skills and teach you how to truly love, to be patient, to have hope, to seek the good of someone else, to forgive.

And even in the messiest relationships, even when a relationship is unhealthy, when we give it over to the Lord, He will make something beautiful out of it. Not that He'll bring you guys back together necessarily (and I don't think you should get back together if it has been unhealthy), but God will heal your heart, shower you with grace, mature you, and use your story to help and comfort others. Because isn't that what grace is all about? Isn't that what our lives are all about? Once we let go and run into the arms of God, He changes our stories into something beautiful.

I personally needed to learn that breakups do not equal failure. I remember feeling embarrassed going anywhere, having to tell people about the breakups, or having to endure their stares or pity looks. I remember feeling completely undone. Messy.

Vulnerable. Naked. But I also remember the community I had surrounding me, hugging me, pulling me close, and letting me cry on their shoulders.

The late-night talks.

The early-morning conversations.

The words of hope.

The words of kindness and grace.

Sometimes feeling completely undone isn't a bad thing but is the very thing that brings the exact healing and freedom we need, if we open ourselves up to Jesus.

Whatever your story is—whether you have had a track record of unhealthy relationships, recently broken up with someone you were with for years, never dated, or dated but it just wasn't the best—Jesus makes all things new. He covers you with His love and forgiveness.

My relationship with Jeff was unique in that we dated, broke up, and then ended up married. When I broke up with Jeff, I wasn't totally sure why I was doing it. I just felt like it was the right thing to do, and I really did think I was obeying the Lord. I can't really explain it other than that in that moment, I knew I was laying my dreams and hopes in God's hands, giving up Jeff, and trusting Him.

I didn't know if we'd ever get back together. I honestly didn't think we would. I wanted to multiple times, but I just didn't see how it could work out. I knew though that either God would do His work in us and bring us back together, or He had someone even better suited for me. My love story was in His hands. I could trust Him to write a good one.

I clung to Job 42:2: "I know that you can do all things, and that no purpose of yours can be thwarted."

I knew that even though I had broken up with Jeff and we were living two thousand miles apart and didn't know where we'd be a year from then, God could still bring us back together. Nothing can stop God's plan. But at the same time, if we weren't supposed to be together, then nothing I did could make us stay together.

Breakups are really opportunities to trust the Lord. If you know it's not best to be together, that this isn't the person you'll marry, if there are red flags, or you both just need to have some space, do you trust God? Are you obeying His voice? Open up your hands, and let Him have His way in your life. Don't hold your love life in your fist anymore. Give it to the Lord. Offer it up freely. Offer it as a sacrifice. And let Him be the author of your story.

TAKEAWAY

None of our relationships or breakups are in vain. God, in His might and goodness, can use them to mature us and make us more whole and holy. Our love stories are in His hands. We can trust Him to write good ones.

WE ARE NEVER EVER GETTING BACK TOGETHER

(Taylor Swift)

"Jeff, I'm already dating someone else."

Those were hardest words I'd ever had to hear.

I've never experienced the death of a close family member or heard a doctor say I had a life-threatening disease, so I can say, without a doubt, those words from Alyssa were the most painful I'd ever received. Probably one of the most soul-crushing moments of my life. I felt mentally paralyzed and stunned.

To convey the weight of the story, though, I need to give a few quick background details. Alyssa had broken up with me about four months before this phone call. She'd broken up with me after a two-week mission trip during which she had "heard from God." Classic, right? For the love, at least give it a few days and think about it. When you come home from the camp high, just make sure it was really God and not the hot dog macaroni and cheese speaking to you. (By the way, if you do hear from the Lord, then *do* what He says.)

Alyssa would probably say that was her way of letting me down easy rather than telling me she didn't like me and didn't see herself marrying me. But sometimes a "God told me" card can make it worse. Because it makes you feel like the other person has Skype access to Jesus while you're still on that flip phone mess. Did she hear something I couldn't?

The breakup was valid, though, and completely needed. Looking back, I realize I hadn't been following Jesus that long, so I was still very much in the middle of rearranging my life around my new Christian identity. I still needed to work through a lot of baggage, specifically in regard to past relationships. Alyssa was older than me, had been a Christian for a lot longer, was out of college, and had a job. I was not quite as mature yet.

During our relationship, I was terrified of rejection, which showed itself in a lot of unhealthy ways. I had never risked or led or put myself out there in a relationship—which were the very things she was desperately looking for me to do. I was afraid of failure or her not liking something about me. I was never honest with my words or vulnerable, because I was afraid she would break up with me. Isn't it interesting how the things I was doing to *prevent* Alyssa from seeing the real me became the things that led to the breakup? Because of my self-preservation mode, I sometimes came off as cold, distant, emotionally guarded. So when she broke up with me, I realized I had some serious work to do.

Even after four months, I wasn't over Alyssa. I knew she was still the girl I wanted to marry. And I started doing the hard work to change the things she broke up with me for. But change doesn't just happen. Even though it's fueled by grace and we can't lose that, it also takes hard work. It's a wrestle, and sometimes that leaves you bloody, bruised, and shaken up. But that's where healing comes from. I had found healing in places I needed to, and I started to understand what it meant to risk and that there is freedom in Jesus to do so.

One day I decided to do the very thing she had been wanting me to do. I was going to call her and just put it all on the line. So I texted her and asked if we could Skype. When she agreed, I called her.

It's important to note that I had a journal full of everything I was going to say. I said "I love you" for the first time. I told her I wanted to marry her. I told her I'd move to Hawaii for her. (Which, while it was a big deal for me then, was actually dumb to say. Oh yes, I would be really *suffering* by being willing to live in the most beautiful place in the world. *Epic fail, Jeff.*) I probably talked for twenty minutes straight, saying everything I had always thought but never said out loud, as well as all the things I thought she wished I had said the first time.

Pro tip: if you ever find yourself in a similar situation, let the other person talk first.

After my twenty-minute speech, I thought was going to win back the girl of my dreams, but Alyssa paused and said, "Jeff, that's so sweet. And great. And nice. But . . . I have another boyfriend. I'm already dating someone else."

I was horrified, embarrassed, confused, upset. I think I felt every negative emotion possible for humankind to feel in those first few seconds.

Yet I also understood that no matter how she responded, *I had to say what I needed to say.* I *needed* to do it. For love to be love, there has to be risk. There has to be the possibility of rejection.

Now, this hasn't always been the case. There was a time before there was rejection. Before there was hurt. Damage. Pain. Sorrow. Breakups.

It goes back to that fateful day in the garden of Eden. When God made humankind, and put into motion the first love story in all creation—the story of male and female. He gave them a job to do: "Go create beauty and order just like I did, and have a lot of babies to help you" (my paraphrase, obviously). In order to do the job well, they needed to lean on their Creator for wisdom and guidance and help and intimacy. And He told them that they shouldn't eat of this one tree put right there in the middle of the garden, the tree that would give them wisdom and knowledge on their own—without their Creator. So it was their pick. Have God be God, or be their own gods.

They picked the latter. And everything shattered.

No longer creation, but now decreation.

No longer life, but now death.

No longer a garden, but now a desert.

And ever since then, the curse has spread all the way down to this very moment. After Adam and Eve ate of the fruit, ultimately the relationship God centered the world on—the marriage of man and women—was the very place it broke down so enormously.

No longer one.

Divided.

Shame-filled.

Hiding.

The place sin entered the world first was a marriage. It's as if the evil one knew how important a marriage is to God's story. And now that very image that perfectly reflected the goodness and graciousness of their Creator became a broken mirror. They distorted the image, and in a deep irony, the fracturing of our parents' humanness was passed down through the very thing that was meant to show what true love is—children.

Our parents knew true love but then lost it. We are born without it, and we start searching for it the day we take our first breath. And from that moment in the garden on, love—true love—has been distorted, and stepped on and marred and broken. The word *love* now carries thousands of years of baggage that betrays its meaning to most of us.

The biggest temptation is to start thinking love is what we think it is or what we have already experienced, rather than what it was created to be, rather than what we saw happen on a hill two thousand years ago outside Jerusalem. Because that's the love that can save us, and that love has a face—Jesus'. Where we were no longer left guessing. Where the very God of the universe who John claims *is* love, entered into our story. And laid down His life in order to draw us to Himself. Not to force. Not to coerce. But to woo. That's love.

Even though a very lucrative movie industry would like you to believe it's true, I don't believe in "the one": the idea that there is one person chosen for each of us. Love is not a fairy tale. Sure, it *was*. But since the third chapter of Genesis, love became much more than that. Even Hollywood knows this. In all the classic fairy tales, the movie ends the minute real life starts. As soon as the couple finally commit to each other or start their life together, the credits roll.

I'd love to see a movie that starts, not ends, after that moment of commitment. And one that shows the fights, the arguments, the stress, the hurt, the pain, the chores, the exhaustion, the frustration, the bills, the complacency, and on and on and on. And *then* see the credits say "*happily ever after.*"

Because it's in those moments that reality starts to collide with the dream we've envisioned, and a lot of times, we have a full-blown crisis because we thought that person was "the one!" So many of us spend our whole lives looking for the one. But little do we realize, "the one" is a myth perpetuated by Disney and romantic comedies, not by the Bible.

How did I know Alyssa was the one? Because *I married her.* She became "the one" the minute I committed my life to her. I know it's really unromantic, but Alyssa and I agree that we both could've married someone else and probably been totally happy and had a great life.

It's not about finding the mythical magical unicorn but about finding someone who will be a great partner for life. And frankly, "the one" doesn't really make sense from a logical standpoint. All it would take is for one guy fifteen hundred years ago to marry the wrong person (not the one for him), and he would create an endless cycle all the way down to you and me, since he married someone else's "the one" and so on and so on.

Though we don't like to admit it, trying to find "the one" stalls growth in ourselves, because our idea of "the one" essentially becomes whoever will make us change the least or whoever is so perfectly suited for us that we don't need to grow, learn, or change.

It also crushes the other person because no one can carry that weight. People disappoint each other and hurt each other, and we all have struggles and sins. Being another person's savior is a crushing calling. Only Jesus can handle the weight of that burden, and when we understand the weight of our expectation, it frees us *and* the other person to become who God wants us to be.

In God's providence, there is a certain level of weaving and moving and bringing two people together. If you're not already married, it's possible God has someone for you who you might not even know yet. So we have to be careful. Alyssa and I have seen people justify divorce because, well, their spouse just wasn't the one. For Alyssa and me, it was incredibly freeing when we realized that there were plenty of people we could have married, but we *chose* each other. That's what matters.

I'd love to see a movie where at the altar the two people say, "I could marry someone else, I don't believe in the concept of 'the one,' but I do believe in choosing one person to love and serve for the rest of my life, and I choose you."

But that'll never happen, because that's boring (and kind of unromantic). But the truth is, true love *is* boring.

> True love is doing the laundry when you usually don't, because your spouse needs a break.

> True love is *choosing* to love even when you don't feel like it. *Every single day.*

> True love is saying sorry for the one-millionth time.

> True love is always searching for ways to serve the other.

Boring makes for a crappy movie but a great marriage. Love isn't a fairy tale, and it isn't about finding Prince Charming. The beauty and sacredness—and the difficult part—about marriage is that the moment you get married, you start to see little by little how the other person *wasn't* that Prince Charming (or Princess Charming? We need better fairy tale names) you thought he (or she) was. And that's where the real joy kicks in. In the trenches of the messiness.

•

One of the worst things that can happen in a relationship is *expecting* the fairy tale and getting something else. That doubles the toughness of marriage because, well, *you didn't sign up for this.* Which ties closely to another thing love isn't.

Love isn't a feeling. Sure, you'll feel butterflies. Sure, when you're dating, just one glance at the person and you probably feel like you're about to faint. But those feelings aren't love.

I was in an airport recently and was lying down on the chairs, trying to sleep for a few hours during my layover after an all-night flight. If you've ever tried that, you know it's an impossible task. Nonetheless, I tried.

Because my eyes were closed and I looked like I was sleeping, I think the people next to me, an older couple, probably figured I wasn't listening or didn't care. They appeared to be in their sixties and probably had been married for thirty or forty years, and they were talking with a woman who was about thirty. I could tell they had just met at the airport and were getting to know each other. Somehow the topic of marriage came up, and the younger woman mentioned that she was just recently divorced. The older couple asked why, and she responded, "My husband and I just weren't happy anymore."

While people divorce for myriad reasons, her reason that they weren't happy anymore really stuck with me. Happiness is a feeling. I feel happy sometimes. I don't feel happy sometimes. Sometimes very legitimate things make me happy. Sometimes those same things don't make me happy at all. It's a fleeting feeling. A similar reason is to divorce because you're not in love anymore. And I don't fault the lady one bit, because she's just doing exactly what our culture *tells you* is the right thing to do—that to follow your feelings is the most important thing.

But to end a marriage because you're not in love anymore is like selling your car because you ran out of gas. You don't sell the car; you fill it back up. You take care of it. You take it in for maintenance and checkups. You renew the tabs just like you renew your vows. Love isn't a feeling; it's a commitment. And one follows the other. Commitment is more like the car, and feelings are more like the trailer. You can't get anywhere with a trailer. But if the trailer is hooked up to a car, it goes where the car goes. If commitment drives the car, then the feelings will probably follow. But if the feelings drive the car, you'll sit in a parking lot all night wondering why you're not going anywhere.

The older couple sitting there listened to her for a while, offered an "I'm so sorry," and then politely encouraged her. But I opened my eyes briefly and caught what I think was a little twinge in their eyes. A little hint of "oh, honey, marriage isn't about happiness."

They had been married longer than I have been alive, and I'm sure they had moments, if not months or years even, when they weren't happy. When they fell out of love. When there were hard seasons. When they probably thought ending it was better than fighting for it.

No one gets a fifty-year marriage because it was easy.

No one gets a fifty-year marriage because they "stayed in love."

No one reaches their fiftieth anniversary because the butterflies in their stomachs got them there.

It's why the psychologist Paul Tournier said, "I've been married seven different times. All to the same woman."

While he never got divorced, it was his way of saying that his marriage continually morphed and transitioned, and that change can't be a reason for divorce. (Please know that I'm not talking about toxic elements in a marriage, like porn, adultery, or abuse. Not the same at all.)

One thing I hear a lot, similar to the conversation I overheard at the airport, is, "Well, my wife isn't who she used to be. I woke up one day and realized that she wasn't the same person I married." It's then that they think, "The marriage must be over, because my spouse is no longer who she was when we agreed to this commitment."

What I want to emphasize is that sometimes your spouse becomes someone different. In fact, the truth is, your spouse is *always* becoming someone different. People *always* change. I'm not the person I was five years ago. Heck, I'm not the same as even one year ago. All of us are always changing and pursuing and growing, hopefully for the better, but not always. And the commitment we make at the altar encompasses those changes. It says, no matter how much *we* change, the promise won't.

If love isn't a commitment, then what's the point of the vows we say? Unless "til death do us part" really means "til the feelings go away."

●

For the majority of my adolescence and young adult years, I had predicated my life on doing things that made me the happiest, put me in the best position, and felt the best for me. My actions and decisions were dictated by that principle. Plain and simple selfishness. And it played out in relationships too. Starting from high school onward, I treated relationships as if they were simply there to serve me. Give me what I wanted. Make my life easier.

Of course, I don't like admitting this or saying this out loud. But that's how I lived. And we all do it, to some degree. Love, to us, is about *us*. But by its nature, selfishness cannot coexist with true love. We all know we can't just blatantly be all about ourselves. It has to be slyer; otherwise our relationships wouldn't get past the first day. So we subtly play the game. Deep down, most of us know that even the "nice" things we do for others are done, in part, so that we might get something in return.

In an incredibly raw and vulnerable article titled "I Don't Owe Anyone My Body," author Kirsten King recounts going on two dates with a man named Tim after being matched on Tinder.[1] After multiple failed attempts by Tim to hook up with Kirsten after the second date, pressure that some ladies know all too well, he finally got the hint, yet walked out in anger, saying, "I mean, I took you to drinks and a concert. Most guys wouldn't go through all that effort for some random girl."

While that's an extreme scenario, many of us do similar things but with much more subtlety. It's what we do in an argument with our spouse about some menial task around the house—when we bring up all the other stuff we've done for them in the past.

Or it's that subtle whisper in our heart that usually starts with, "But I . . ." *But I took out the trash and washed the dishes, why can't she just give me a break? But I have worked hard and saved hard. I deserve that new car or new toy even if she doesn't think so.*

Love isn't entitlement. It's not doing something for someone so you can get what you truly want.

So then, what is it?

It's seeking the highest good of the other. Love is elevating another person above yourself. Love is Jesus. Or a better way to say that is, if you want to know what love looks like, look to Jesus. Look to that Jewish rabbi, who claimed He was God, who spent every ounce of energy poured out for others and for God. Who loved until it hurt. Literally. Who was nailed to a piece of wood between two criminals, brutally tortured and left to die. Who was innocent, and yet suffered as if He weren't. Who died, so we could live. And who, in the very moment humanity was doing its very worst to Him, spoke the most tender words anyone could speak, especially given the context: "Father, forgive them. They don't know what they are doing."

A man who was pleading for a people's forgiveness the same minute they were spitting on Him, hurling insults, and laughing at Him. When I finally understood this, it changed me. It changed how I pursued, loved, and risked for Alyssa.

When we first dated, I was so young in following Jesus that I hadn't worked through a lot of things, especially not risk or truly understanding what love really is. I wouldn't risk or put myself out there, because I was afraid of rejection and being hurt. Yet during our breakup I realized risk is the very essence of love. A *going first* mentality is critical to love, rather than *Oh, let's wait to see what they do first, so I can respond and not look dumb or get hurt.* I also didn't realize love was about commitment, not feelings. About promise, not pleasure. About covenant, not contract.

And the reason I realized this better the second time around is because I decided to look to the source.

We aren't left guessing. We know what love is. Because, better yet, we know *who* Love is.

TAKEAWAY

True love involves incredible risk. If you want true love, you have to be vulnerable. If you focus on protecting yourself from possible hurt, then you'll never know the depths and joy of love. They go hand in hand.

Love is primarily about serving the other person. We don't always know how the other person will respond, but we do it because Jesus first loved—and served—us.

IF YOU
WANT
TO KNOW
WHAT
LOVE
LOOKS LIKE,
LOOK TO
JESUS.

10

WHEN I'M 64

(The Beatles)

When Alyssa and I first started dating, I was terrified—terrified I'd ruin it. Terrified she'd see the real me and run. Terrified because I had never done a relationship the right way before.

My journey to follow Jesus led me to clearly see that I had been approaching relationships all wrong. No wonder they had always ended badly and affected me so severely. So I put a lot of pressure on myself when I first started dating Alyssa. I quickly realized, however, that it all came down to a proper vision and boundaries. So many of us, myself included, get into relationships with no vision. We never ask ourselves:

Why am I dating this person?

Where is my relationship with this person going to take me?

133

Does this person make me better or worse?

Are our gifts and talents better together than separate?

If we asked those questions before we got into a relationship, we'd probably be in a much better spot (I know I would!). A lot of times, though, those aren't the reasons we get into relationships. Many begin with lust or infatuation, which basically describes every relationship I had before Alyssa.

But Alyssa and I decided early on to be incredibly clear and intentional. That meant I told her I only wanted to date her if I could see myself marrying her—and I could see that with her. Now, of course I wanted to get to know her better. I wasn't interested in getting married anytime soon, but marriage was the vision.

I don't necessarily think you should date every person with the goal of marriage. I think that's the problem sometimes with Christian culture, especially at Christian universities, where girls are terrified to go out for coffee with guys because the next day the whole campus will think they are getting married by the next end of next week.

So quick word of advice to the fellas. Have purpose and have vision, but don't make it weird. It was just friendly conversation over a cup of coffee. *Be normal* are probably the best words of advice I could ever give to a guy in his twenties who wants to date.

Alyssa and I first spent time together getting to know each other. I saw how she was in group settings with other friends, what she liked to do for fun, what her goals were in life. Those are great things to find out *before* jumping all in. Building a friendship is a great first step.

It's also a good idea to see how the person treats others. That's a great indication of how he or she will treat you two to three years from now when the puppy love wears off. Ladies, here are two quick thoughts. First, watch how he treats his mom. That's exactly how he'll treat you if you marry him. Is he kind, respectful, generous, compassionate, and loving? Also, imagine your future son turning out just like your husband. If that thought makes you cringe, you probably should break up. But if it makes you excited, that's a good sign.

Once Alyssa and I realized we seriously liked each other and wanted to give this a shot, we made it clear we wanted to date with a vision. I saw so many of my friends—including myself, for many years—completely underestimate how affected their hearts and emotions and longings and desires and everything in between were by going down the muddied path of "just hanging out" with someone we liked but it was going nowhere. It's naive to believe we can enter into a noncommittal, flirty, romantic relationship with someone and not have it affect us. If a relationship has no vision or purpose or goal, then it certainly will negatively affect both people. And the hard part is that our culture has exacerbated this. Girls and guys have to read between the lines far too often.

We live in a world where texting someone and asking them to hang out is code for "let's date," but we want to be so noncommittal and ambiguous in our language that if anything happens, we word it just right so we can say we never even dated or we didn't really care anyway.

I know this, because that was me for years. Getting what I wanted out of relationships with the least amount of work and vulnerability not only hurt the other person but almost destroyed me. Decayed my humanness. While it looked like it was just me trying to feel powerful and in control, it in fact was me being completely dominated by fear.

Eliminating all risk is an easy way to eliminate all hurt. But eliminating risk is also the sure way to eliminate true love and joy and harden a heart.

I haven't seen many relationships end in hurt or confusion because the two people *over*communicated. But I've seen dozens that were left in shambles, and affected the people in future relationships, because of *under*communication.

Rule of thumb: Don't play games. Be up front. Be honest.

I recently heard someone say, "Dating without the intent of marriage is like going to the grocery store with no money. You either leave unsatisfied or take something that isn't yours." While I don't think this quote is a perfect metaphor, the point remains that dating without vision usually only ends in confusion and hurt.

Having purpose and vision matters, especially because the foundation we lay is the foundation we build our lives on. This is why the beginning of a relationship is vitally important. Whatever we set as the foundation of that relationship will ultimately be what that relationship builds on going forward. We need to ask ourselves, what is the best foundation?

If you're making out 90 percent of the time you're together, then that becomes the foundation of your relationship.

IF YOUR MARRIAGE IS JUST ABOUT YOUR MARRIAGE, IT'S PROBABLY NOT GOING TO LAST.

If you're looking at porn while you're dating someone, that becomes the foundation of your relationship.

If you date with purpose, vision, and integrity, then that becomes the foundation of your relationship.

In fact, if you do the last one, you're setting yourself up well for marriage, where a vision and purpose isn't just a nice, cute thing, but a complete necessity. A marriage without purpose is hardly a marriage. Another way to put it: if your marriage is just about your marriage, it's probably not going to last.

Of course, even if you don't know where you're going, you can still be driving in the right direction. But a map and a vision and a finish line make for fewer detours, fewer roadblocks, and less waste of gas.

Here are some great questions that usually act as a good guide in determining whether or not a relationship is a good one.

> Will this person expand, grow, and help facilitate the vision and call God has put on your life?

> Will whatever you feel led to do with your life be better or worse with this person?

And here's why it matters so much: if you get married, it becomes arguably the most powerful agent to shape you into who you will become. I always find it strange when I hear Christian people talking about what it means to be a Christian and they say things like attending church, being "holy" (which usually means separating from all the "bad" people), singing Christian songs, and being as spiritual as possible.

But, that's not what it means to be a Christian. To be a Christian means to be a follower of Jesus and to be an image bearer. When you're being a good image bearer, you're following Jesus well.

A lot of us are trying to be angels—not humans. Angels are not image bearers. When you open up Scripture and read about angels, what are they usually doing? Worshiping. Singing praises. Kneeling at His throne.

But God gave us humans *jobs to do.* Prayer and worship are vital but certainly not the core of what it means to be human. What it means to be human is to create, to cultivate, and to come alongside the work God is doing to build His kingdom.

A common misconception about the beginning of Genesis is that the whole world was beautiful and tamed and looked like the garden of Eden. But some scholars believe the garden of Eden was relatively small, and outside it the earth was wild, untamed, and a little more chaotic. In fact, that is one of the basic premises of Genesis: God is creating order out of chaos. And calling us to do the same. God gave humans the garden as our blueprint. He points to the garden and essentially is saying, "Go make the rest of the world look like this. Bring it under your rule. Go garden."

Gardening, at the fundamental level, is taking raw materials and making something beautiful and useful. In a literal sense, that means to take raw materials—seed, soil, water—and grow food. Give people life. In a metaphorical sense, all of us are gardeners. Artists take paint, brushes, and canvas and make something beautiful. Musicians take sounds and instruments and make incredible music. Olympians take weights, nutrition, and training and create awe-inspiring routines. They are "gardening."

That's what the first marriage was created for. And every human—married, dating, or single—is part of this grand call. To go out and create and cultivate. To hone a craft. To be part of a bigger story. It's no coincidence that in the same verse in which God commands Adam and Eve to subdue the earth (Genesis 1:28), He tells them to be fruitful and multiply. They were given an enormous task—to make the rest of the world orderly and beautiful, and to subdue it. And that task is still unfinished. Marriage and work, from day one, have been a fascinating, intertwined relationship.

Everyone, single or married, is a gardener. In fact, I think the apostle Paul even makes the case in some of his letters, that being single frees you up in more ways than a marriage does to *do exactly that.*

Single or married, we need to ask, *what's our garden?*

Alyssa and I answer that question in many ways and keep that question in front of us so we don't wander aimlessly through our marriage. The way we most often examine where we are is by writing down or thinking of words that resonate with us in the season we're in: *generosity, hospitality, family, writing, teaching,* and *marriage* are just a few of the words that represent things we feel are our "garden" right now.

Generosity. We are compelled to be generous in this season in a different way than the standard tithe. So every month, we put aside money until we hear of a need or God lays someone on our hearts. This could be pitching in for a crib for friends, helping out with some friends' adoption process, or surprising a couple with a hotel room, a dinner gift card, and an offer to watch their kids. All just because that's the garden God has given us at the moment, and we want to steward and cultivate it well.

Hospitality. We believe home is sacred and that meals around a table are a peculiar, beautiful moment when heaven and earth collide, and we are reminded of the table Jesus so graciously invites us all to. It's why we try to Sabbath once a week, when we turn off our phones, eat a good meal, and celebrate what God has done for us. And we rest. It also means we try to have people over a lot. And sometimes it's inconvenient. And sometimes it means pizza and paper towels and paper plates. But rarely does someone remember the food; almost always they remember how they felt and how they were treated.

Take an hour with your boyfriend or girlfriend or spouse. Go grab an Ethiopian single-origin pour-over cup of coffee (okay, maybe that's just me—shoutout to my fellow coffee nerds) and a notebook, and dream and pray and laugh and shoot for the stars. You'll be surprised at what comes out simply when you set the table and ask the questions.

In fact, this is pretty much how every good business I know operates. It's why I always find it a little peculiar in the Western American culture how well we do business in this regard and how poorly we do marriage, family, other relationships. For example, it's not uncommon for businesses to have a laser-sharp focus and vision. If a business doesn't know why it exists, then it probably won't be in business for long. And to affect others, the *why*—not the *what*—is the most important.

It's also not uncommon for a business to have a mission statement. Or to do quarterly review meetings. Or a yearly retreat, when they look back on the year and rest and plan for the next one. And there's lots of talk about "company culture."

That's why Google headquarters has slides and bikes and ball pits. My favorite paddleboard company, Tower, has a five-hour workday policy. Pixar allows *any* employee to give criticism after the screening of a rough film cut, when most studios only allow executives to give feedback on film edits. Joe Biden famously sent out a memo to his White House staff telling them they'd better not miss any birthdays, anniversaries, graduations, or other special days for work-related things. In all these examples, companies and individuals aren't just setting rules or making the office fun—they are creating a culture. And culture matters. The culture you create and foster is ultimately what you become.

And just as in a business, this intentionality in dating, marriage, and families takes time, cultivation, and planning. What would it look like if all through the years, the family was a nucleus, an incubator of ideas and goals and dreams and visions?

Develop your own weekly rhythm to check in with your partner. Make sure you're on the same page. Make sure you have goals—one might be just to get to know the person you're dating. Make sure you find mentors, people who are ahead of you in life, people you can look up to. Make sure you're using what you have to make a difference in those around you and in your circle of friends. Whatever it is, be intentional.

•

A marriage that is intentional is a marriage that will last, a marriage that will, over time and with hard work, see each other's talents and gifts intertwine beautifully.

The coming together of two souls, man and woman in an eternal covenant, is about more than just butterflies in the stomach and a nice romantic feeling. It's about the redemption of the world—and it has been since day one.

Marriage is one of God's main ways not only to communicate to the world about Himself but also to put the world back together. Marriage is about gardening. In the very beginning, in Genesis 2:15, God put Adam and Eve in the garden of Eden to "work it and to keep it." They had a job to do.

To create.

To cultivate.

To build.

To *work*.

Notice that God blessed Abraham, which led to him becoming a blessing for others (all of Israel, in fact). We are blessed in order to be a blessing. God puts two people together, not for themselves, but so they can love their neighbors, serve their community, and live their lives in fellowship with those around them.

TAKEAWAY

One of the best ways to guarantee relational health is to make the relationship proactive, not reactive. Create a vision and set goals for your relationship. Decide to Sabbath. To go on date nights. To give money to those you know need it. Invite your neighbors over for dinner. Let your relationship be an intentional blessing to others.

AT LAST

(Etta James)

On April 29, 2012, I traveled with Jeff to a church in western Washington. I was so excited to spend the whole day with him and to hear him speak. He was gone so much during that season in our dating relationship.

The night before, we had attended a friend's wedding. For some reason, I thought he was going to propose that night. I don't know why. It just seemed right. We were in pre-engagement counseling. His friend who does all his videotaping was in town, so I knew that if he wanted to film it, it had to be *this* weekend.

I had my nails done. I was ready. But that night, as we took a break from all the dancing and walked hand in hand outside on the golf course, Jeff began asking me about rings. What kind I liked. What cut. Then he said the horrible words: "I don't get what the big deal is with diamonds. Why would you spend all that money for a real diamond, when you could get a fake one that's gorgeous for way cheaper?"

I immediately stopped walking and felt my heart sink.

This guy doesn't even have a ring for me. He's not ready to get engaged. It's not happening.

I cried myself to sleep that night. Which sounds a bit dramatic, but I had my heart so set on something, my hopes so high, and it all crashed down on me. I was devastated. I was so ready to marry this guy, and now I believed it wasn't even on his radar. (Side note: Guys, most girls want a real diamond, no matter how small. And this girl right here, definitely wanted the real thing!)

All that is to say, I was excited to see Jeff the next day, but I had to wear a bit more makeup than usual to cover up my puffy eyes. We drove up north, where he spoke at a church. Afterward, the pastor and his wife invited us to go out to lunch with them, and if you know Jeff, then you know he never turns down an invitation for food. But he said we couldn't. I was so confused. We had nothing going on. Why not go out to lunch? When I asked what we were doing, Jeff told me he had planned a picnic lunch for us, so we weren't able to tag along.

Then he started sweating.

As we were leaving, he told me we were going to Gig Harbor for our picnic and that he had a special spot in mind. It sounded wonderful. When we finally got there, my tummy was rumbling. We walked down a grassy knoll streaming with white daisies to a path along a wooden fence. Then I noticed there were candles lit all along the way, rose petals scattered everywhere, and pictures of Jeff and me from the time we met to just the month before.

This was it!

This was the moment I had been waiting for. We stopped and looked at each picture, my hands shaking with excitement and my stomach full of butterflies. As we reached the water, there was a blanket laid out for us, surrounded by candles and rose petals. We sat down, and Jeff began to tell me how much he loved me and how he didn't want to live without me for one more day. I felt so loved and known. And then he got out a bowl and a thermos of hot water and began to wash my feet.

Jeff told me he wanted to spend the rest of his days serving and loving me. I probably should have had tears streaming down my face, but I was so completely happy that all I could do was smile. I had always dreamed of my future husband washing my feet when he proposed to me, but had never said anything about it to Jeff. That this was part of his proposal confirmed that he was the man for me.

Finally, he pulled out a ring and asked me to be his wife, to do life with him and be his forever. Without even looking at the ring, I said, *"Yes!"* A million times, *yes*. I couldn't wait to be his forever.

As soon as I said yes, Jeff's two best friends hopped out of the bushes, running toward us with cheers of excitement. They had filmed the whole thing! We popped open a bottle of champagne and I finally looked at my ring.

Gorgeous.

Stunning.

And *real*! (Way to throw me off, Jeff!)

Afterward I woke up every morning thinking, *One day closer to marrying my best friend.*

And for a couple of weeks, I was useless at work. Completely.
I would just sit in my office chair, and stare at my ring. Pinterest
was my best friend. Thankfully, my boss understood and gave me
grace those first couple of weeks.

Every day after work, as I drove home, I would talk to God and
thank Him for this gift and for answering my prayers. Tears would
run down my face because I was so in awe of God's faithfulness
and goodness to me. All those years of hoping, dreaming, and
waiting. All those years of praying for my future husband and of
asking God to please bring me a man who loves Him. Those
wobbly years of dating Jeff, then breaking up, then dating again.
They had finally all come to this point where my hopes became
a reality and my dreams came true. It wasn't perfect, and we
certainly weren't perfect, but I can confidently say that it was
better than anything I had imagined or prayed for.

Because God's in the business of doing just that.

Of showering us with His extravagant love.

Of giving His children good gifts.

Our wedding verse was Isaiah 30:18: "Therefore the LORD waits
to be gracious to you, and therefore he exalts himself to show
mercy to you. For the LORD is a God of justice; blessed are all
those who wait for him."

Jeff was just what I needed. Not that he completed me in any way;
I was complete in Christ. But he complemented me, and we were
better together than apart. Where I was weak, Jeff was strong.
He encouraged me, prayed for me, listened well, and made me

laugh like no one else could. And he loved Jesus deeply. He was humble, gracious, compassionate, and courageous. I knew life with him would be anything but boring, but at the same time, I'd be well taken care of. I knew we would go and do whatever God called us to do, because Jeff was close to the heart of God, and he willingly walked the adventure God had for him.

I couldn't wait to start my life with this man!

Being engaged was so much fun for me. With Jeff, I loved planning our wedding, gathering things for our new home, doing premarital counseling. I loved that it was intentional, purposeful, and we had a specific date. We were engaged for a little less than six months. I have no idea how we pulled off a wedding in that time, especially considering that Jeff was gone a lot, but we did! And I don't think I could have been engaged one day longer. I was so ready to marry this man.

•

One of the reasons dating was so hard for me was because I never knew how long it would go on. When I first became convinced I wanted to marry Jeff, I didn't know where he stood regarding marriage. *Was he ready? Would he pop the question soon? Would we end up spending the rest of our lives together, or would something happen and it not work out?* Being engaged was so sweet because we knew exactly where we stood. We knew where we were going. And finally we were a true "we," a forever "we."

I think knowing our wedding date made the whole temptation thing way easier too. Jeff and I wanted to wait until our wedding night to have sex. We knew that was best, and that's what God calls us to as believers. When you're dating, that can be so hard, and for some engaged couples, it's way too easy to choose not to wait until marriage. But for Jeff and me, knowing there was a countdown actually helped us to wait. We knew we weren't going to have to wait forever.

And if I'm honest, we didn't really have time to be tempted while we were engaged. It was one of the busiest times for us; we didn't see much of each other. Jeff was writing a book and traveling the country like crazy. The month before we got married, I only saw him, like, three times. When we did hang out, we were always with people. Our counselors, our family, our friends. We also weren't together alone at night, since we both had to get up early in the mornings. Not seeing him much was rough—I missed him desperately—but it was refreshing not to have to deal with the physical temptation.

Having clear, set boundaries made the temptation level go way down. Not that it wasn't there, but it was so much easier. It's helpful to surround yourselves with people. And to avoid having late-night "chats" in the car and being out late at night.

An older couple from church invited us to their house for dinner every other week for premarital counseling. We would catch up on life, the wedding plans, and the plans for after marriage, and then dive into our study. We went through Timothy Keller's *The Meaning of Marriage* and talked through topics like personality traits, money management, and sex.

I looked forward to these visits because I was interested in hearing from an older couple who loved us and wanted the best for us. They never played devil's advocate or took sides. They genuinely loved us and encouraged us to be a team. Jeff and I had talked a lot about these things before we got engaged, but having a sounding board and the assurance that we were going in the right direction was very encouraging.

This also gave us a great opportunity to work through disagreements. I remember a handful of times when we were at that dinner table and I tried to hold back tears because Jeff and I disagreed. I mean, those topics you disagree on are huge, especially when you're talking about getting married, which is why it's helpful to have an older couple mentor you—not just during your engagement but throughout your marriage.

It's important to have a couple you both trust so that when you disagree, you can turn to them and they can help you see the situation in a different light. We also talked through things like cleanliness, finances, and conflict, which are, *ahem*, "fun" to work through still today in our marriage.

We talked about where we were going to live and about Jeff's traveling. Jeff had always wanted to live in the inner city and do ministry there, but I hadn't realized that he wanted to pursue it after we were married. Though we had a lot of talks about this with our mentors, the decision ended up being an easier one than we thought it would be. When we were looking for a rental in a sketchy part of Tacoma, Jeff found a beautiful Craftsman home, but it was right next to an abandoned home and a crack house. No wonder the price had been so low! Because Jeff was traveling a lot, he said he wouldn't feel comfortable leaving me at that house.

Yes, Jeff wanted to live in the inner city and serve the people there, but when it came down to it, we realized that wasn't what God was calling us to as a couple or as a family.

IT'S HELPFUL TO HAVE AN OLDER COUPLE MENTOR YOU—NOT JUST DURING YOUR ENGAGEMENT BUT THROUGHOUT YOUR MARRIAGE.

I also had a hard decision to make regarding work. I knew that when we got married, I would either keep my job and be home alone a lot or quit and travel with Jeff. While I wanted to quit and be with Jeff, I struggled to let go and take a leap of faith. I enjoyed being a high school counselor and needed the money until we got married, but I knew that traveling with Jeff would be the best thing for our marriage.

I was excited to just be with him, but a big thing we wrestled over during our counseling was how to travel together. Jeff was frequently asked to speak, and sometimes I felt left out or like I didn't have any say in the response. We learned to talk about each opportunity and to decide what was best for us as a couple. Should we accept the speaking gig or stay home? We were entering each other's worlds, and it took a lot of time and counsel to know how to blend our lives together.

This certainly doesn't mean our marriage was problem free that first year, but it gave us a really good foundation. It helped us to get on the same page, to have the tools to talk through issues when they came up later, and to prepare for our life together. This also was the couple we turned to that first year of marriage when we did have conflict and needed a third party's advice. We knew they were for our marriage and weren't going to pick sides. They loved both of us, fought for our marriage, and provided a safe place for us to talk through anything.

So while I enjoyed planning our wedding (well, technically, I had started planning when I was two years old!), I also had the opportunity during this season to look forward to spending my life with my best friend. Engagement is a great time to look back on God's faithfulness and rejoice at the story He wrote just for you two. Bringing two people together to show His love to the world is a crazy gift.

TAKEAWAY

Being engaged can be fun, but it takes a lot of time and counsel to learn how to blend two lives together in marriage. Seek counsel to help your relationship flourish and grow.

12

STAY WITH YOU

(John Legend)

Did you know Jesus only *directly* answers a question seven times in the Gospels? Out of all the times Jesus taught, responded to a critique, began preaching, and so on, you can count on both hands the number of times He gave a direct answer. Most of the time when He was asked a question, He responded with a story, often called a parable, or with another question, which is why Jesus is the original, and way better, Yoda.

One of my favorite times when He did this is during an exchange with the Pharisees, recorded in Matthew 19. The Pharisees were the most religiously devout people of the day. They had memorized entire Old Testament books. They had rituals and rhythms that would put even your varsity Sunday school Bible memory person to shame. In regard to religious holiness, they crushed it.

They came to Jesus and asked, "Is it lawful to divorce one's wife for any cause?" (verse 3).

Jesus could have responded with a simple yes or no. Or He could have answered with precise clauses that allowed for a divorce. But Jesus, being the Jedi ninja He is, didn't want to give them exactly what they wanted—and we want—a hard and fast rule, devoid of life.

We are often addicted to rules and knowing where the line is. Rules makes life easy, as they're tangible and measurable. We know exactly when we break a rule or cross a line. In reality, we don't need Jesus if rules are enough. If they could do the job. Jesus understood that a direct answer would have fed only these professional rule followers' desire for a precise ruling.

What *does* He say? He actually doesn't talk about the law at all.

The Pharisees were calling on the power of Moses the minute they asked, "Is it lawful?" They wanted to have a gotcha moment, pitting Jesus against Moses. But Jesus didn't defer to the law. He deferred to *the beginning.*

He skipped right over Moses and went even *further* back. To the first page.

Jesus asked, "Have you not read—," which would have been a great way to start an answer to the most well-read and well-versed people of the first century. They most likely even had it memorized. Basically, Jesus dropped the mic on people in His first sentence.

But He went on and said, "Have you not read that he who created them from the beginning made them male and female, and said, 'Therefore a man shall leave his father and his mother and hold fast to his wife, and the two shall become one flesh'?

So they are no longer two but one flesh. What therefore God has joined together, let not man separate" (vv. 4–6).

The Pharisees wanted to talk about the law; Jesus wanted to talk about creation.

The Pharisees wanted to know the rule; Jesus wanted us to know God's heart.

Understanding this is important because when we concentrate on the rule, it not only can get us stuck in the weeds, but it can also lead to a really low view of marriage that brings no life, joy, or intimacy.

It's also why we see some weird things in Scripture like polygamy, concubines, incest, and other things that would have surpassed most reality TV shows. But in Jesus' answer, we see a clear statement that just because it's in the Bible doesn't mean it's the right thing. Some parts of the Bible are descriptive, but that doesn't mean they are prescriptive.

We have to always dig, always search, and always ask, "What's God's *heart* on this matter?" Not just the rule. Because if you live by the rule, you can do that without Jesus. But you can't know someone's heart without *knowing* them and being in relationship with them. And that's what God wants—for our marriages and relationships to be fueled by our relationship with Him.

Notice how Jesus upholds a high view of marriage, which is polar opposite to that of the Pharisees'.

They described marriage as simply a contract. A piece of paper.

"Why then," they asked, "did Moses command that a man give his wife a certificate of divorce and send her away?"

But Jesus said marriage is about *oneness*—a complete unification of two separate entities. A piece of paper and "one flesh" sound like two very different things. And frankly, the English translation *one flesh* used in the Genesis verse fails us. The English language can only do so much, and sometimes the original languages had meaning and words for things that are hard to capture in our language.

That word for "one flesh" in Hebrew is *echad*, and it literally means "to fuse together at the deepest parts of our being." That when we step into marriage, we are so fused together, we can't be taken apart.

●

My first job was flipping burgers at McDonald's. And while I didn't love that exact job per se, I was thankful for it, and I got my fair share of free fries. I learned a lot of things during my short time there, like the importance of being on time for your boss, how to interact with fellow employees, and the basic structure of an employee-employer relationship—I offer my services or time or energy, in exchange for monetary value of sorts.

The big mistake a lot of us make in our relationships is that we treat them no differently than our jobs. But a job is a contract relationship, while a marriage is a covenant relationship. And there's a big difference between the two.

A contract is about the behavior, not the promise. You mess up bad enough, you're fired. See ya later. Give me your name tag back. Please turn in your uniform too.

But a covenant is about the promise, not the behavior. Meaning, the thing that holds the relationship together isn't the behavior of the two parties, but actually the promise the two made.

There are only two covenant relationships—the parent-kid relationship and the husband-wife relationship. And guess what two examples are primarily used to describe God's relationship with us in Scripture? A father to his children, and a husband to his wife.

If God loved us and pursued us based on a contract, He would've thrown in the towel a long time ago. We haven't cut it from day one. But it's about His nature (or promise), not our behavior. We can't earn it, and we can't lose it.

We aren't His slaves; we are His children.

A covenant has a way of creating an entirely different relationship than a contract does. Because a covenant is the only thing powerful enough to house the full you. The true you. The naked you. The person you don't want anyone to see, know about, or find out. Because in a contract, you know that if you share too much, a person could leave.

What if they knew about my past?

What if I mess up bad enough in the present?

But in covenant you are free to drop the act, lower the guard, and be truly vulnerable. And when you're vulnerable, true love comes flooding in.

You can't be fully loved unless you're fully known. And you can't be fully known unless you're fully loved.

And that's the game many of us play in relationships. We think, *If they knew the real me, they'd never want me.*

So we keep up this act.

Put on the mask.

Build up a facade.

Hop back on the treadmill. (By the way, could there be any better analogy for this than a treadmill, aka the worst thing ever invented? You are literally sweating, working, and trying your hardest *just to stay in the same place.* No, thanks.)

But deep down, when we are lying in our beds at night, we know. We feel like a fraud. A fake. And part of us is terrified. Nothing is more terrifying than being truly *seen.*

All the hurt.

All the shame.

All the fragments.

All the fears.

All the thoughts.

So we hide. But from the beginning God's voice has been calling us out of hiding, into intimacy, and a marriage that's full of life is a marriage that models that. It says, "I see all that you are and see you for who you really are, and I still want you. I'm not going anywhere."

Instead, many of us find ourselves in marriages that feel more like jobs. When we mess up, we are called into the boss's office. A full-blown performance review is held, where we hear how bad we've messed up, what's wrong with us, and why we aren't fit to be a good spouse.

And sadly, looking back on my experiences, it's easy to see that I was bringing a lot of that into my marriage. I was insanely competitive as a kid and on the baseball field. I was the kid who turned *everything* into a competition or debate. I wanted to *win*.

When I started to follow Jesus, I began to see just how hurtful I was being, all in the name of winning an argument. And in marriage, that is poison. A marriage in which one or both spouses care more about winning is a marriage that won't last.

Because in a marriage it's not about winning arguments; it's about winning the person.

Alyssa is my best friend and wife, not my competition.

In a contract you are always trying to outdo the other person, because a contract is usually about protecting yourself. But a covenant is about giving yourself.

A contract is about self-preservation. A covenant is about self-denial.

The more I dug into my own heart, and the more I was exposed in marriage, the more I realized I was a slave to fear in many ways. That protection of "I'm right, you're wrong" was coming out of a place of fear. And covenant and fear don't mix well. Because there is no fear when you know that the covenant of love is the sustaining power of the relationship.

•

When Alyssa and I were first married, I began to fear. *What if I mess up this whole marriage thing? What if I make one stupid mistake that totally devastates Alyssa?*

Sometimes, even now, my inner demons create a monologue in my head that says, *Nice try. You've had a good run at this good husband and father thing, but you know who you truly are.* I know my past. I know my proclivities and temptations and weaknesses. And sometimes that can cripple me. I breathe the fear almost like oxygen.

And guess what? Those thoughts became the *reason* I messed up. I feared failure, and in a vicious cycle, when I did that, I failed.

We call that a self-fulfilling prophecy. When you start to believe something so much that it becomes true. My fear of failing is actually why I would fail.

The Devil's biggest tool is to get you to believe lies about yourself. If he can do that, he can destroy you. If he can do that, you'll take care of the rest. Because we only act out of who we believe we truly are. And if the Devil can get you to believe certain things about yourself—that you're no good, you're worthless, you don't deserve a good marriage because of your past—then you'll start to spiral downward. And live as if that were true.

But the beautiful part is, truth is always more powerful. Always.

It's just sometimes a little quieter than the lies. So we have to listen. And tune our hearts and ears to the voice of Truth. But even though that voice might sound like a whisper sometimes, it holds more weight. It is truth. It is life.

I can't even begin to describe my indebtedness to Alyssa and just how much she is the very grace of God manifest to me. She knows me. She knows my temptations to get in a mental spiral. To have bad days of fighting shame, and past sins and images and thoughts. And she'll look me straight in the eye, in a piercing way, and simply say, "That's not you. That person is dead. That person was buried two thousand years ago outside Jerusalem. That person was united in Christ's death *but* also united with Him in new life. Jeff, you're new. A new creation. A new person. A new legacy. Walk in that."

And I can't tell you how many times that has brought me back. The shame washes away. The fear dissipates.

One of the biggest mistakes we make in a marriage is in those moments when we hide. We don't let our spouse in. We try to cover it up. But that actually prevents intimacy in marriage. Hiding is the death blow to intimacy.

True joy and love and intimacy are found in the moments when we *want* to hide but expose ourselves to each other anyway. It's in those moments of vulnerability we knit a love that lasts.

And it's in those moments that the receiving spouse has the ability to create life or death for the relationship. He or she can create one of two trajectories. If they receive that vulnerability with grace and love and tenderness, then, multiplied over the years, that creates more and more intimacy and oneness and closeness. But if they receive the vulnerability with condemnation or indignation

HIDING IS THE DEATH BLOW TO INTIMACY.

or frustration, then, over the years, that creates a chasm that sends the other spouse more into the cave of their heart, where they hide and cover up and only put their best foot forward.

Never forget that in a marriage you have the ability to create life or death for the other person, specifically with your words.

●

The other day I walked into our bathroom, and Alyssa had written a "10 Things I Love About You" list on the mirror with dry erase marker. It listed things like "I love how you see the home responsibilities as a team effort" and "I love how selfless you are" and "I love how you draw me out with kindness."

But the reality is, those things aren't always true about me.

Alyssa isn't lying, though. Rather, she's speaking life and truth over me. And in a weird way, guess what happens? They more and more start to *become true.* She's speaking an identity over me that I then step into.

This is the joy and beauty and amazingness of the marriage covenant. Since we are closer to our spouse than to anyone else, our words have the greatest impact. And when we step into that gift, we can continually breathe life into each other.

But the opposite is also true, and we must also be aware of how powerfully our words can hurt our spouse. And this is primarily because of the closeness. For example, some guy who cuts me off in traffic can call me an idiot or a poor excuse for a man, and I probably wouldn't care one bit. With my personality, I'd probably chuckle and then feel bad for the guy. But if Alyssa called me that? I'd be *devastated.*

The words didn't change, but the person who spoke them did. And this matters.

Our words have weight, and never more so than in marriage. So let us be people who build each other up, who breathe life into our spouses, who only let encouragement, kindness, and gentleness fall from our lips—especially to the person we've entered into a covenant with.

Because in those words and in our actions, we can slowly allow all our *contract* perceptions to fade and know we are entering into a *promise*—and that's where joy is. And in that promise, we don't need to fear, because fear is the opposite of love.

TAKEAWAY

A marriage covenant reflects God's relationship with us. Because He has promised to stay with us forever, we can be vulnerable with Him. In marriage we need that same comfort and security—the freedom to share our hearts with each other without fear of rejection. And when we are truly vulnerable, true love comes flooding in.

13

ALL OF ME

(John Legend)

The summer after we got married, our adventure of making YouTube videos and writing books took us across the world to Germany, Uganda, and London, and we even decided to add in a weeklong trip to Italy. We visited a castle in Germany where Jeff spoke to thousands of youth leaders through a translator. (It was so much fun to watch a translator keep up with Jeff!) Then we spent two weeks at an orphanage in Uganda eating mangoes from trees with the kids, visiting people in their huts who were dying of AIDS, and singing worship songs with all the employees and children at the orphanage.

We'd had an amazing trip so far, and before we went to London, we were so excited to go to the land of pasta and vineyards and romance. We had all our hotels booked, trains scheduled, and adventures mapped out. A few days into our Italian visit, however, it turned sour, fast.

Jeff started to feel not-so-hot, and needed to stop at a bathroom every thirty minutes. I was a bit impatient with him. I mean, I spent months planning for this trip, and now the guy wasn't up for all our plans? Then, about eight hours later, it suddenly hit me too. I climbed into our bed in Montepulciano, shaking uncontrollably, and started bawling. I hadn't felt this bad in a long time. I started to google what to do (never a smart idea!), and after I researched online, it hit me: we had malaria! I was convinced we were dying. We would never make it back to the States. We were going to be stuck in an Italian hospital for months.

"Jeff, we have to go home. We're so sick. We have malaria. I know it. Can you check flights out? Can we skip London, tell them we can't make it? We have to get home."

Thankfully I'm married to a very sensible man, who convinced me to take some heavy medication and try to fall asleep. "You'll feel better in the morning," he said. Well, I didn't feel better the next morning—or the morning after. But eventually we did start to feel better (we just had the flu), although we stuck to a bland diet of spaghetti and french fries for the rest of the trip.

The last place we visited was the Amalfi Coast, which is the most beautiful and romantic place I've ever been. Love is in the air. We hopped on a tour bus to take us to our hotel, and for two hours I was glued to the window, in awe of the scenery. The road runs along a massive cliff that jets down to the water, and all we saw around us was this gorgeous, green cliff and water for miles. Little homes and restaurants set into the mountain, old-fashioned umbrellas surrounding the beaches, a soccer field built on the rooftop of a building, and little cars zooming past on the other side. I felt like I had traveled back fifty years and was in a Cary Grant movie.

When our bus pulled up to our hotel that afternoon, we heard music blaring from the courtyard and saw a hundred people sitting around tables, eating and celebrating. An Italian wedding! The bellman showed us to our room, which was a little apartment built right into the cliff. We had a balcony all to ourselves, and all we could see was the water surrounding us.

Then we entered our room, and as the day became night, we heard *boom! boom! boom!* We looked at each other and scurried back onto our balcony. Bright colors flashed before our eyes, filling up the entire sky. Obviously the fireworks were for the newly married couple, but from where we stood, we couldn't see anyone. Just us, the ocean and moon, and the huge firework show. We held each other close and just stood there in awe.

I wish I could say our entire first year of marriage was as romantic and magical as that one night. We had a lot of those moments, but we also had some hard things to walk through. Our first year of marriage was a roller coaster. We had so many adventures and made incredible memories. We traveled all over. Jeff spoke at churches and conferences. We led Bible studies and helped lead a college ministry. We moved twice. Each of us wrote a book. In addition to all that, we got pregnant. (Surprise!)

And we were learning how to be married. How do we communicate and work through conflict? What are our roles? How do we balance traveling and working from home and leading a ministry? How do we each believe the best about the other person and yet not have expectations that will leave us discouraged? And then there's sex–oh, and in-laws.

The first year of marriage can be hard, as it's foundational to the rest of your marriage. There's so much to work through and so much that you're learning about each other. And it's also probably one of the sweetest times because you just married the love of your life. No wonder it was customary in the Old Testament for the Israelites to take the whole year off their first year of marriage.[1]

•

I felt as though I had to really learn who I was and what God was calling me to do. For so long, I had hoped and dreamed about being a wife. I read countless books, listened to sermons, and learned from older, godly women. I knew in my head how to be a wife, but experiencing it firsthand was a whole different thing. I knew I should submit to my husband, but what did that look like? I knew I should serve him with joy, but when I was exhausted, I just didn't want to. I knew I needed to pray for him, be patient, and talk through things using kind words, but in the heat of the moment, I just wanted to either slap him or run away bawling.

I learned a lot that first year. I came into marriage not realizing how much pressure I had put on myself to be the perfect wife. I quit my job a few months before marrying Jeff, and I thought that since I didn't work outside the home, I needed to make everything perfect inside the home. The house needed to be spotless. I needed to go to the grocery store on Mondays, find the best deals, and make every meal from scratch. Oh, and those meals had to be vegan, a whole new way of cooking that I wasn't used to, because Jeff had decided on our honeymoon to change up his diet after watching a Netflix documentary.

There always needed to be fresh laundry, folded and neat. And don't even talk about inviting people over for dinner or to stay with us. I would crumble over my need to be perfect, paralyzing myself with decisions about what to prepare and how to make sure they had everything they needed. *This is my job,* I told myself. *I need to be perfect for Jeff and for everyone else, and I want to prove that I am a godly wife.*

I remember one particular day when I'd been putting myself under this intense pressure. I'd been at home cleaning. I had myself on a tight schedule. I still had to vacuum the floors, clean another bathroom, and finish the laundry. Then I needed to get dinner started before Jeff got home. As I was scrubbing the toilet, tears welled up in my eyes. "I can't do this, Lord. It's too much. I really don't know what I'm doing, and it feels so heavy."

But the Lord drew me close and whispered to my fragmented heart, "Alyssa, you don't need to be perfect. You don't need to earn My love or Jeff's love or anyone else's approval. You are mine. I love you for you. Jeff loves you for you. So live in freedom, live in the rhythm of My grace."

I learned that part of being a wife is creating a safe haven for your husband. But you have to ask questions, give it time, and get to know what details make your home a place of refuge for *your* husband. A picked-up house is really important to Jeff. He likes everything to be in its place. He loves having people over but also needs a good amount of time to be by himself, or with just our family.

I learned more about what my husband needs, and I also learned my limitations. We have a house cleaner, and at least once a week we get take-out for dinner because I sometimes just can't get a hot meal on the table. We talk about our plans for the week, about who we want to get together with, but also when there will be time for just us at home to get recharged.

I'm still learning how to make our home a refuge, and I'm discovering that it changes as our family grows and changes.

I accepted the grace I needed and learned that just because I was a stay-at-home wife, I didn't have to run myself ragged. The Lord gave me the opportunity to be at home, and if that meant I wanted to read a book all day, I could do just that. I could rest. Never before in my adult life had I experienced that freedom. I had always been working or involved in ministry and felt like there was always more to do.

Finally I was at a place where, if I didn't have anything pressing to do, I could rest. And in fact Jeff wanted me to rest. He wanted me to be free to do what I wanted to do. To take time to be filled up and refreshed. Sometimes the godliest thing we can do is to rest. To take a nap. To read a good book.

I also learned that marriage is about relying on each other. You're a team, and you're one. When Jeff and I were dating, it was easy for me to get away with hiding my feelings. Not that I was deceitful, but I could hide my deep-down feelings from Jeff, process them alone, and then, if I had to, come and talk to him about it. There were many nights when I went home and cried myself to sleep over a comment that was made or how I interpreted a situation. Sometimes I would bring it up and talk about it with Jeff, and other times it was just something I needed to talk about with the Lord.

But either way, Jeff never saw me cry. He never saw how pained I was. I mean, the night before he proposed, I had bawled myself to sleep thinking he'd *never propose*. That next morning when he picked me up, I'd worn extra makeup to cover up my puffy eyes, and he'd said, none the wiser, "Wow, you look beautiful. And different. Did you put on more eye shadow today?"

When you're married, however, you can't hide anymore. Yes, there will be times when you sneak away and cry alone and process. (Although those times are more rare for me because Jeff works at home, and he's super intuitive.) But at the end of the day, you both sleep in the same bed. There's no more crying yourself to sleep. Your husband is right there, and he wants to talk things through with you. Hear your heart. Process it together.

I usually hate it in the moment, but really, I think that's what God desires in our marriages. We're one now. We're called to bear each other's burdens, to share our hearts, to listen and encourage and speak life into each other. To pray for each other, to ask for forgiveness, to ask for help. No one knows you better than your spouse does. You take care of each other.

•

I learned that first year that I chose well when I married Jeff. We definitely had our arguments, but I always knew that Jeff was faithful. I could count on him. He was never going to leave me. He fought for our marriage. He fought for us to reconcile, to find healing and wholeness. Every time we argued, as he still does to this day, Jeff was the first one to come to me and ask for forgiveness. (I'm really prideful, y'all.)

Within the first few months of being married, we had one of our biggest blowups. I don't even remember what it was about. I slammed the door and went to clean the bathroom, because that's how I dealt with arguments back then. (Now I just go get some chocolate!) I cried the whole time I cleaned. I prayed, but it was more like a heated discussion with God.

"What did I get myself into? Why did I marry him? Who is he, anyway? God, what did I do?"

After a little bit of time, Jeff came knocking on the door and made me sit down. He gave me the biggest hug, and asked me to forgive him, saying he shouldn't have said what he did, he shouldn't have used that tone, and he was so sorry. And I remembered right then why I married him. Because he is humble, and his humility is one of the things I love most about him. Even when I'm the one primarily in the wrong, he always admits his sin first. I don't know if you can have a healthy marriage without forgiveness and grace at the forefront. Because the reality is, we're all sinners, and relationships are messy, and we can hurt each other so easily. But there is an abundance of hope and joy when we are humble and extend grace to each other.

●

Marriage is so much fun when it's with your best friend.

When our first Christmas came up, both Jeff and I were excited, and we went to a Christmas tree farm to cut down our first (and last) Christmas tree. (Who knew it was so much work to get a real one?) We decorated the house and planned parties, and I picked out exactly what I wanted for Christmas—a yellow lab puppy with a big red bow. I was only joking though. Kind of. I had always dreamed of getting a yellow lab puppy with a big red bow, since watching the last scene of *Miracle on 34th Street*. But I knew that a puppy wasn't practical for us at that time. We were traveling all the time, and our landlord had a strict no-pet policy. But I'd still lie in bed at night, showing Jeff pictures of puppies.

One night I was busy cooking dinner, and Jeff texted me, asking if I could go up to the attic and look for something. As I was rummaging upstairs, I heard him come home. I found what I was looking for and ran downstairs to meet him. And there, under our (hard-earned) Christmas tree, was a yellow lab puppy with a big red bow. Jeff was standing next to him, with the biggest smile on his face.

Fast-forward a few weeks, and we were in full potty training mode. Aslan was pretty good about going outside, but one afternoon he was super quiet, so I looked over from my laptop to see what he was up to, and there on our carpeted floors, was a pile of poop. I freaked. I had no idea what to do. All I knew was that I had to discard it immediately! I ran into the kitchen, grabbed as many paper towels as possible, and went in to swipe it up. But now there was just a pile of poop in my hands. I ran into our bathroom, but Jeff was there.

"Jeff, move, move! Aslan pooped, and I have poop in my hands! I have to flush it down the toilet!"

"Babe, I can't do anything right now. I can't move. I'm literally pooping."

"You have to get off! I have to get rid of this!"

Silence. Glare.

"Babe! *Move!*"

He lifted one cheek. I plopped Aslan's poop in the toilet and flushed.

Mission accomplished.

And Jeff went back to his business.

Marriage is crazy good, crazy hard, and crazy fun. I always had a picture in my head of what marriage would be. I'd be married to my best friend (who'd be crazy good-looking and Jeff is definitely that), and we'd have four kids and a dog. We'd laugh all the time together, have long heart-to-hearts, and hold hands wherever we went. He would go to work during the day and then come home to me cooking dinner, wearing an apron, and I'd run up to him and give him a big ol' kiss. We'd never fight or argue, because we would always communicate perfectly.

You know what? Our marriage looks a lot like that. I married my best friend, and we laugh a lot. We have a lot of heart-to-hearts, although not all the time. We have two adorable kids and a crazy dog. However, dinner prep usually looks like me in the kitchen with dishes and food everywhere, our toddler going through all her clothes and her brother's clothes and strewing them all over the floor, and our little boy rolling all over the living room and getting stuck under the couch.

There's usually a lot of talking and crying and an occasional tantrum—sometimes from one of the kids. And Jeff and I do argue. We don't always choose Jesus or choose each other. We can be selfish, impatient, and short with each other. We get tired and misunderstand each other. We're not always jiving, as I like to put it, not always on the same page, or even on the same team.

MARRIAGE IS CRAZY GOOD, CRAZY HARD, AND CRAZY FUN.

So while marriage isn't exactly what I thought it would be, it's a lot better than I thought. More real. More life. More forgiveness and grace and healing and joy. We're human and therefore messy. But by God's grace, we're growing and learning about each other. Learning how to serve each other, how to communicate better, how to put the other person above ourselves.

We're learning to embrace the chaos, because in that we see Jesus a lot more clearly. We need Him more, and He is proven to be strong and wise and so gracious. Grace upon grace. I love how marriage draws us closer to each other and closer to Jesus.

TAKEAWAY

The first year of marriage can be a roller coaster. Relationships are messy, and we hurt each other easily. But there is an abundance of hope and joy when we are humble and extend grace to each other. Marriage draws us closer to each other and closer to Jesus.

14

LET'S GET IT ON

(Marvin Gaye)

Sex is everywhere. I see it on the magazine covers when I check out at the grocery store, it seems like it's all that's talked about on TV, and the majority of people are thinking about it 60 to 90 percent of the time. While everyone's experience with sex is different, I would argue that regardless of where you fall on the spectrum—multiple partners, living with your boyfriend or girlfriend, abuse, porn, going to third base, or falling on the other side of the spectrum as a virgin, never have kissed someone, wearing a purity ring—we all need healing in some way in this area.

Somewhere along the way our thinking got warped. All of us, in some way, don't know God's full vision of sex, or we may know it, but it hasn't infiltrated our hearts and brought us to full flourishing.

Having grown up in the church and in the era of the purity ring and saving yourself for marriage, I thought my view of sex was 100 percent spot-on. I thought I had this thing down. I mean, I hadn't even held a guy's hand until I was twenty-two, and that was my husband's! But after Jeff and I got married, I realized that the world's idea of sex had slipped into my thinking and was affecting our marriage. Sex was a challenge. I had some misconceptions that I needed to get rid of, and I needed to let God breathe into me His idea of and desire for sex.

When I was about thirteen, I read a book by Jaci Velasquez in which she shared her testimony of how she came to know Jesus. Toward the end of it, she shared how she had decided to wait to have sex until she got married. She even wore a ring on her ring finger, a purity ring, to remind herself of this promise. I loved the idea.

I was just entering puberty and knew my heart well enough to know that I could easily see myself down the road having sex with a boy I really liked. But when I read what Jaci wrote, I knew that God had something better in store. I knew that if I waited for my husband, I would not only be obedient to the Lord, but it would also be the best thing. And I wanted the best. I wanted to obey the Lord, and I wanted to do it His way.

When I turned fifteen, my parents bought me a purity ring. They wrote a letter along with it and made a special dinner. It was beautiful. Gold with diamonds and two sapphire hearts (for my September birthday). They shared how their hope and dream for me was for me to wait to give myself to my husband. I was so thankful for parents who wanted the best for me and encouraged me in this area.

And so I waited. Which, as you know, wasn't so hard, considering I didn't date anyone until years later. I think, though, that having made a promise to God and to my parents and to myself helped me to have high standards for the guy I wanted to be with. It helped me to not settle for just anyone, because I was saving myself for *someone*.

This promise didn't just involve my body, however. It also was my way of promising God that I'd fight to stay pure in body and *mind*. God's desire for us is to walk in purity. To not lust with our eyes. To not fantasize in our minds, which was something I had been addicted to before. I wanted to be holy, because God called me to be holy. Not that I could do it on my own at all, but through His Spirit in me, I could choose to think about something else when temptation came my way. When I was tempted to undress a man with my eyes, or when I wanted to fantasize about what sex could be like, instead I chose to honor guys, to treat them as brothers, and to see them as image bearers of Christ.

When I finally started dating Jeff, and then Chad, I was terrified of sex. I had waited so long for my husband that the last thing I wanted to do was give in and have sex. It truly is hard when you are in a relationship, and even harder when you know this is the man for you. When I was around Jeff, my knees got shaky, my hands sweaty. He gave me butterflies like no one ever had. It was difficult not to jump all over him.

As we dated, the temptation only became greater. We had steamy moments for sure. I would ask the Holy Spirit to come on our dates with us. I knew He already was with us, because He lived inside us, but praying for it reminded me and gave me His strength. Really, it came down to asking myself who I wanted to please—God, Jeff, or myself? A lot of times I chose Jeff and myself. When it was too much, too steamy, too intimate. But God continued to lead us, forgive us, show us His way, how to choose Him above all. We both wanted to do it God's way, and, by God's grace alone, we made it to the altar.

To say I was excited to finally have sex with the man I loved and had committed myself to for life was an understatement. *Finally.* All those years of waiting and hoping were over. I would finally give myself to my husband. I'd packed a whole suitcase of lingerie. I was ready.

And let me tell you, it was good. And awkward and clumsy. And then I got super sick on our honeymoon. (No, I wasn't pregnant. I think it was the guacamole.) Jeff ended up taking me to the doctor before we left for the second half of our honeymoon. I knew my immune system had been down throughout the whole week of the wedding, but I didn't know I had an intense bladder infection. Needless to say, it definitely didn't go as I had planned, but it was still special because it was our story.

It wasn't perfect, and that was okay because we were married and had time to learn together, to figure out what we each liked and didn't like, what worked and what didn't. We were learning how to serve each other, how to put the other person before ourself, how to please each other. I remember feeling lame for getting so sick, but Jeff just held me and told me it was okay. He took care of me and was totally content to just rest and hang out.

It was the first time I had to really rely on Jeff, and I saw how blessed I was to be married to him. He was just what I needed. He just went with the flow and was thankful, gracious, and content. No pressure. No need to perform. He just loved me for me, and took care of me so sweetly.

SEX IN MARRIAGE IS A WAY OF REMEMBERING OUR VOWS TO EACH OTHER.

Sex in marriage is a way of remembering our vows to each other.

It's a recommitting.

Putting the other first.

Serving each other.

Becoming one flesh.

Sex brings a couple together, and I've found that it can take our pulse on how our relationship is doing. At least in my heart. If I'm holding anything against Jeff, if I am bitter in any way or frustrated, when he asks about sex that night, my immediate response is, "No, thanks. I'm tired." And then I'll stop, check my heart, and realize that yes, I'm tired (I'm always tired these days with two kids!), but that's not the reason. The reason is because I was hurt in some way that day and don't want to be intimate with my body.

I may not have realized the state of my heart all day until that question is asked. It provides a good opportunity then for me to go to Jeff and communicate. To ask for forgiveness if need be. To share how I may have been hurt that day or how we miscommunicated, or how we need to just connect on a heart level before we connect physically. Sometimes, though, connecting physically is just what we need, and then that leads to connecting at a heart level. It can be a little complicated! Humans are such intricate creatures. But God is gracious to give us sex to help us reconnect, to help us learn to serve and to be united, in heart and mind and body. And when all those are working on full cylinders, it's incredible. Sex does get better and better as you grow together.

Before we got married, I read *Intended for Pleasure*, which was a great book on sex, written from a doctor's perspective.[1] It helped me to understand all "the parts," so to speak. I came into marriage thinking that if I followed all the steps, sex would be amazing every time. And it's not. Sometimes it's a five-course steak meal, and other times it's a quick trip through the McDonald's drive-thru. Sometimes it's beautiful and unifying, and other times it can end in hurt and miscommunication.

Knowing all the parts is good, but sex is more like a dance. Sometimes you step on each other's toes and run into each other, and other times you're so in step and get a perfect ten score. It's a giving and a taking.

I've found that, for me, my mind is the main part in sex. If I'm thinking of Jeff, how thankful I am for him, how proud I am of him, sex is beautiful. I feel God's presence there. I know how delighted He is in our union. But if I'm distracted by other things—the kids, what we're going to do tomorrow, what I still need to do today—or if I have any distortions about sex, it quickly goes downhill. Sex is a time for me to just focus on Jeff. To put him first, to just be with him and enjoy.

But sex has also been a struggle at times, especially during that first year of marriage. I began our marriage excited and giddy about sex. I had high expectations for my first time. I thought it'd be amazing every time. I thought we would do it every day, maybe more than once a day. I thought it'd be like in the movies. But it wasn't.

I found myself pursuing Jeff, planning ahead, thinking about it all day, and Jeff didn't. He was tired a lot. Often when I'd ask, he'd ask if we could do it another night. When I would pursue, he'd say he just couldn't that night. Not always, of course. But there were more nos than yeses. I felt rejected. Unwanted. Less than. I feared asking and gave up hope, because I didn't want to feel rejected one more time. As the dinner hour would get close, I would tell myself to not have any expectations, because it might not happen tonight.

Not wanting to get my hopes up. Not wanting to get hurt anymore. Trying to protect my very vulnerable heart. I felt lonely. And so discouraged. We would argue. How could I feel so lonely and hurt, when this was supposed to be the best time in my life?

I met with a mentor. I read books. I prayed and gave my frail heart to God. Jeff and I tried to talk through it all the time, but it just seemed like we weren't getting anywhere.

Finally the year came to a close. We moved to a quiet place on the lake, twenty minutes away from the city, and suddenly our sex life was amazing. Beautiful. We were loving and serving each other. No more feelings of rejection or deep hurt, only love and grace. And then I understood, and so did Jeff.

The first year of our marriage had been so busy. We traveled so many miles. Jeff spoke in a crazy amount of places, not to mention that he finished writing his first book and helped start a college ministry. He was discipling guys for our college ministry, we had gotten a dog, and we had an exchange student live with us. Jeff was supporting a wife, figuring out finances, figuring out how to lead our home.

He had done a great job, but when he decided to step down from the college ministry, it was like a huge weight had been lifted from his back. All together, it had been too much. He was exhausted from trying to juggle everything, and he had been feeling that he couldn't give his best to anything. But now that he was more free, he was more at peace and was feeling like he could give his best to his commitments, including sex. He wanted to be with me, often. Suddenly, it felt as though it was just the two of us out on that lake, and we were able to really pursue and know each other. We became best friends again, able to be intentional with each other.

We became a family in that lake house. As life slowed down a bit for us, Jeff was able to assess his heart. He realized that although he had healed and found freedom from his broken past, and although he had formed a good theology about sex before entering marriage, his past had still affected him that first year in ways that he hadn't realized. After getting married, it was as though he had a whole other level of healing to walk through. He had to fight thoughts about the past, put off shame and guilt, and accept that it was good to desire sex again, because now it was in the way God intended.

After having our daughter, and while I was pregnant with our second baby, we faced another difficult period. But this time, our roles were reversed. Jeff was the one feeling hurt and alone, and I was the one fearful and tired all the time. After I had our daughter, my body took a long time to heal. Sex was painful, and I feared getting pregnant again. I also feared being too tired to be up in the night with a new baby.

Then, when I got pregnant again, I just plain ol' didn't want to have sex. Jeff felt rejected and hurt, and rightly so. We had to work through my fears together, learning a whole new dance. And

I had to go to the Lord, and ask Him to reveal things in my heart. To help me to change. To serve Jeff through sex, even when the feelings weren't there.

I started to pray for Jeff more intentionally, through a book called *Praying for Your Husband from Head to Toe*.[2] Each day, there's a part about marriage and sex. I found that as I prayed through Scripture, and prayed those prayers, my heart toward sex changed dramatically. I'd been seeing it as a service I *had* to perform. (Maybe moms tend to think that? When the sparks of marriage dwindle a bit, the tiredness sets in, and the constant pouring ourselves out to our kids comes into play, moms can begin to think of sex as a job.) But after my prayers, I realized it was a gift I was blessed to give Jeff. It was a way to show him I loved him, a way to reconnect and recommit. It was such an honor to be able to make love with my husband, and I wanted to revel in that.

I'm so thankful to have a husband to be intimate and completely vulnerable with. No one else knows me like my husband does. There's no shame. No fear. We're one, and we're learning to become more and more united in body and soul. And as we do, we're becoming more and more whole. God is slowly healing our hearts from the past, from misconstrued ideas and perceptions.

Sex forces us to have hard conversations, to be honest and gracious and forgiving. Nothing else reveals my selfishness like sex does. Because the thing is, sex isn't about what you'll receive. (Which I often wrongly think.) It's about what you can give. How can you serve your spouse? What do they like? How can you show them you love and desire them in this moment? It's having sex sometimes when you don't feel like it or think it's inconvenient, because it serves the other person.

It's strange how that happens. Before you're married, all you want to do is jump your boyfriend or girlfriend, but then when you get married, it changes. It's like Satan does everything to tempt you to have sex before marriage but then everything to stop you from having sex after you get married. And then, when you have kids, it's a whole other thing you have to work through in your marriage.

As much as I love sex, I often dismiss it or forget to think about it in the midst of everything else going on. I get so busy with the kids and my to-do list that it doesn't cross my mind or I don't plan ahead for it, and I'm too exhausted. But I'm learning to plan ahead, to think about it, to be excited about it. Sometimes that means an easy dinner and skipping the laundry so I can have more energy at the end of my day. Sometimes that means going out and buying a piece of lingerie and putting it somewhere Jeff will see it.

I'm also learning to *see* my husband during the day. Sometimes I get so busy that as soon as our kids wake up in the morning, I'm running with my day all planned out—nap times, mealtimes, things I have to get done before the time of day I know the kids will have a meltdown. Jeff will joke around in the kitchen or use sexual innuendo that the kids won't understand, and I'll just ignore him because I have things to do!

The other day, we weren't on the same page and kept butting heads, so Jeff stopped me to do a fifteen-second kiss. (Our friends who run a marriage ministry suggest that you give each other a fifteen-second kiss each day because it forces you to stop and just be with that person.) And you know what I did? I pushed him away and told him I didn't have fifteen seconds. How awful! Fifteen seconds was all he wanted, but because it didn't fit into my time schedule, I dismissed it.

Sad thing is, if either of my kids asked me for fifteen seconds of my time, I'd give it to them in a heartbeat. After I pushed him away, we just looked at each other and laughed because we both knew how ridiculous I was being. And then we had our fifteen-second kiss. And it was wonderful. I felt my body relax in that moment, and I was able to notice, be with, and give attention to my husband. And the kids loved it! Kinsley loves it when she sees Jeff and me being affectionate with each other. It gives her security. She knows that her mom and dad love each other, are committed to each other, and that they actually like each other!

Because we do live in a fallen world, sex can be hard and broken, and whatever happens before you get married gets brought into the marriage. But, thankfully, our God is a God of wholeness and healing and freedom, a God of *shalom*, and that's what He's calling us into, and that's what He declares over us.

In her study *Be Still and Know*, Rebekah Lyons reminds us that we have been set free (Galatians 5:1), so we can live freely (1 Peter 2:16–17), and we have been given the Spirit to keep us free (2 Corinthians 3:17).[3] So whatever your story is, whatever your history with sex, and wherever you are now, know that God is a God of freedom, and He is constantly beckoning you to live in His freedom that He paid for on the cross at such a high cost. You are His. Rest in the truth that your identity is in Him, and live in the freedom of a life that pleases Him.

TAKEAWAY

Sex is a gift from God, meant to help us to reconnect, to learn to serve, and to be united in heart and mind and body. Whatever happens before we get married gets brought into our marriages, but God is a God of wholeness and healing and freedom. Our identity is in Him, not in our past.

15

LET'S TALK ABOUT SEX

(Salt-N-Pepa)

One of the more interesting years of my life was when I was a resident adviser my senior year of college. The school was a small, private, secular liberal arts college right outside Portland, Oregon, and about as progressive, liberal, and hippie as you can get. Students wore flannels, drank out of a Nalgene bottles, and talked about the evils of corporations.

And I loved it.

I've always been the type of person who loves being the minority or outsider in groups. I had more non-Christian friends than Christian friends, and I enjoyed hearing other people's views. There was something peaceful and enjoyable about knowing where everyone's views landed, and it was so much different from my time at a Christian school, where the waters were muddier. Were you a Christian because you were raised one? Do you really love Jesus?

I had a viewpoint on sex that wasn't the norm. Well, I mean, in comparison to the school's culture of sex. As an RA, I was expected to put on different programs for our hall—anything from an ice cream social to programs on social media etiquette and security or on one of the more common themes like sexuality.

I remember a particular RA who typed up different sex facts—STD prevention, different positions, fun facts about all things sex-related—and taped them and a condom to each door on the hall.

Or the year before, when I was just a student, another RA, whom I'd never met, came to my door and announced, "Candies and condoms!" Because nothing says Halloween like sugar and latex.

One of the more interesting programs I heard about from other RAs was a sexy scavenger hunt where they basically sent students around campus to find things like lotion, a banana, a condom, and a toothbrush and in return give them prizes and then educated them based on the items retrieved.

Another was passing out candy in a group, then asking everyone to exchange the candy three to four times with three to four different people. After they did that, the RA would tell them that the people they had exchanged candy with symbolized people they had unprotected sex with and that the random candies like Snickers, Jolly Ranchers, and Smarties symbolized STDs, and whoever had those particular candies now had a corresponding STD.

It was pretty clear that the general thinking about sex on campus was that sex was something you *should* be doing. It was recreational, fun, harmless, and great for stress relief—as long as you used protection and didn't get diseases.

In a weird paradox, sex was both everything and nothing, all at the same time.

Everything, because it seemed to be central to people's lives, thoughts, and even social viewpoints. In our culture, sex defines who we are. Our sexuality is our identity.

Professor Jenell Paris writes in her book *The End of Sexual Identity*: "On a personal level we're told that our inner sexual feelings are the measure of our true selves—that by knowing, exploring, and expressing our sexual desires, we become our real selves. Efforts to discipline or redirect sexual feelings for the sake of a greater cause may be seen as foolish or even dehumanizing."[1]

But also nothing, because it was clear that it really *wasn't that big of a deal*. There seemed, in some of the dating relationships I knew at school, to be almost a competition over who could care the least.

I even remember one student comparing sex to a handshake, implying that it's as common and normal as a handshake but a lot more fun and enjoyable. This always struck me as strange, because it's one of those classic worldviews that quickly breaks down once brought into the real world. No one who would claim that sex is "just a handshake" could completely stick to that thinking if their girlfriend or boyfriend decided to go "handshake" with someone else.

But it was clear on campus that sex was both a sport and a religion. I remember having some conversations with friends or people in class about all this. And the conversation would quickly break down and fall into the weeds of categorizing it as right, wrong, liberal, conservative, religious, or nonreligious. It always seemed to spiral down toward someone saying a certain behavior is sin and the other party saying, "That's oppressive."

It was through those conversations I realized we are having the conversation about sex on the wrong wavelength—on both sides. And there are a couple of truths neither side is talking about or acknowledging.

Christians usually react to the hypersexualization in culture by communicating a completely sexless spirituality—sex as the ultimate taboo. Christians who react to sex as *too* big of a deal actually still make it a huge deal, just in a different way: changing it from recreation and hypersexualization to something that is dirty or unwanted and *never* needs to be talked about.

But in some ways, sex really isn't as big a deal as we make it.

The reality is, we are not slaves to our desire. To our sexual feelings. To our sexuality. It's an integral part of who we are, but it does not control us or define us. It is not our identity.

Another way I think we've done a disservice to this issue is by boiling down sexuality to "doing it." We have oversimplified sexuality to basically mean two people's body parts touching.

But in reality, sexuality is so much bigger than that. One quick way to make a twentysomething's jaw drop is to tell him or her they can have a flourishing and full sexuality and never have sex. (Just ask Jesus.)

Sexuality is primarily about intimacy and communal connection. It's ultimately about creating life—in the obvious form of children, and in the less obvious forms of connection, friendship, beauty, goodness, and encouragement.

The word *sex* comes from the Latin word *secare*, which literally means "to cut off, to sever, to amputate, or to disconnect from the whole." We are born into this state—cut off, unwhole, disconnected, and lonely. And life becomes about finding, through various ways, that wholeness, putting us back together.

From the very beginning we ache with separation. We are thirsty for connection. We are starved for intimacy. And that longing, that ache, that call within us—that is true sexuality. It's a gross reduction to say *that* is simply about having sex. It's not.

In his book *The Holy Longing*, Ronald Rolheiser writes, "One can have a lot of sex and still lack real love, community, family, friendship, and creativity, just as one may be celibate and have these in abundance . . . It is painful to sleep alone but it is perhaps even more painful to sleep alone when you are not sleeping alone."[2]

And this matters because the act of sex becomes an overflow of already living with connection and intimacy. And marriage is the only context in which a fire that powerful can be held. Without the confines of marriage, where there is full trust, commitment, and covenant until the deathbed—sex is a lie. A cheap, quick version of proving something—oneness—that isn't really there.

The Scriptures show us that we can live without sex, but we can't live without intimacy. We can live without erotic pleasure, but we can't live without community. Harnessing that truth, harnessing the beauty and fire and grandness of our sexuality, means that when we meet with a spouse in marriage, we are able to love that person better.

Our culture is *dying* for this type of truth, connection, and intimacy. We have boiled sex down to a narcotic, running to it every time we need a hit to numb, suppress, or excite.

When I was in college, it was clear the overwhelming message was that doing what you wanted, when you wanted, was the definition of liberation. But behind closed doors, many people admitted the broken promises of sex.

●

As a senior in college, I had a burden to creatively love my peers and engage them with the radical message of Jesus' love, grace, and forgiveness. I was hosting a weekly Bible study in the lobby of my dorm room, but every week only about three people would come—which is great and awesome and praise the Lord, I know. But I wanted to reach more people, so why was I trying to get them to come to me in a very unfamiliar situation? Why didn't I meet them where they were?

It was in the middle of those questions that I thought of my school's open mic. They held it roughly once a month, and it was always well attended. Probably two hundred to four hundred people showed up, and the whole school was only about twelve hundred students. My initial thought was, *I don't dance, I don't sing, and I don't play an instrument—this could get ugly real fast.* But then I thought about poetry. I grew up in love with hip-hop

THE SCRIPTURES SHOW US THAT WE CAN LIVE WITHOUT SEX BUT WE CAN'T LIVE WITHOUT INTIMACY.

culture and the art of poetry, rhyming, and performance. I'd watched a ton, been to events, just never performed myself.

In my mind, this was very much a one-time thing. Just using the platform and moment to, hopefully, do something creative to reach my peers about sex. It was what most of us thought about all the time, it was what we saw everywhere around us in media and advertisements, and it was also one of our greatest sources of pain, grief, and hurt.

So I wrote the poem called "Sexual Healing" during a couple of late-night cafeteria study sessions. And as the date approached, I almost died of nerves. In fact, I don't remember ever being that nervous before—you know, the "*I think I'm going to throw up and I can't think straight*" type of nervous. I started having these huge visions of people booing me and shouting me down. I knew that in many ways, the words in my poem were a scandal of sorts among that audience—even more so in spoken-word poetry, where you say things sharply for effect.

And guess what happened the night of the event? People actually related to it and didn't boo me off the stage. In fact, the next day, students wanted to chat with me about what I had said. In very much a Nicodemus moment (Nicodemus was a Pharisee, a usual enemy of Jesus, who came to Jesus at night to sincerely ask questions), my peers would ask questions and give me feedback I never would have heard in a classroom setting.

I realized just how hungry we all are—for intimacy, for connection, for life. And how we know deep in our hearts that the current promise of sex isn't cutting it, no matter how hard we fake it. There is a better way. And Jesus is inviting us into it with open arms.

●

I was angry. I mean, like "red face, smoke out of the ears, but keep your cool because you're a Jesus guy" type of angry.

After college, I was venturing into the YouTube world and had one video on my channel. It was a spoken-word pieced called "Sexual Healing," which was actually the poem I wrote and performed at my college (any Marvin Gaye fans out there?). It was a very vulnerable and explicit poem on my journey from sexual brokenness to healing, redemption, and wholeness.

Late one night as I was sitting at my computer, a stranger tweeted me and said, "Look! This big Facebook page posted your video. So awesome!" In the early days, I would get *so* excited about things like this (let's be honest—I still do!) and track down every share to respond to comments. I headed over to their Facebook page, which was an entire group devoted to staying "pure" in regard to sexuality. As I scrolled, another video caught my eye. It had something with "street experiment" in the title.

I began watching. And that's when I started to get furious.

It was basically one of those "man on the street" videos where someone with a mic walks around a downtown setting asking bystanders various questions. A man would hang out by a van on the street, and as people would walk by, he'd hold out two perfectly identical, sealed, clean bottles of water and ask them, "Which bottle of water would you rather drink?"

Most just looked puzzled or confused at the question. To their dismay he'd say, "Actually, hold on," and pause and open the door to the van. One by one a person would hop out of the van and take the bottle of water in his left hand and drink it, drool on it, accidentally spill it, and lick the rim. Then, after a couple of people had done that, he'd turn to the person again and say, "*Now*, what bottle would you rather drink?"

It of course became obvious he was leading them to basically have no option but to say the sealed, perfect water bottle, not the half-consumed, unsealed, drooled-on water bottle. And then the crescendo of the whole video was him saying something like, "Well, that's how your future spouse will feel about sex and why you should wait and not have sex." He was implying that if you had, you were no better than a nasty, filthy, spit-on, half-empty water bottle.

Let me be clear: this is so wrong, and hurtful, and damaging, psychologically and spiritually.

First, who cares if you're a virgin or not? We all are broken and "dirty" in some way. That's why Jesus came. To *restore* us. Heal us. Be with us. Know us. Love us. Who cares if you wore a *True Love Waits* T-shirt or not? You still need Jesus.

You are not damaged goods.

Your virginity (or lack of) is not the most important thing about you.

Sex isn't who you are.

You don't need to marry the first person you date.

You don't need to feel bad if you've heard "sex is bad" all your life and then can't suddenly flip the switch when you get married to enjoy its beauty and amazingness. The weird contradiction of evangelicalism is that it preaches two very different messages. One: sex is dirty and wrong and evil. But two: you should get married so you can do it, because it's awesome.

That message has left millions hurt, confused, broken, and bitter.

And, at least in my situation, woefully unprepared. I tried for years to play the part. Doing what I thought it meant to be a Christian. Especially in regard to sexuality, dating, relationships, and more.

But because I wasn't actually fueled by a relationship with Jesus, because it was just simply me being religious, I was exhausted. It wasn't working. It brought no joy and no life.

So I thought, *Well, maybe it doesn't work. Maybe doing whatever I want is the answer.*

Sex, girls, and the chase consumed me. I can say that now, after looking back, but when I was nineteen, I know for a fact I wouldn't have admitted—or even known—that was why I woke up every morning. But it was what made me tick.

Ultimately it was about gratification. Satisfaction. That brief moment in time when pain, shame, and guilt seem to be a distant memory. Euphoria. That moment of connectedness. A hollow one though. A cheaper one. A bastard stepchild version of true nakedness.

My generation seemed to really get the short end of the stick when it came to relationships, as there were really only two extremes—admittedly stereotypical—when it came to how to do relationships.

The first one is what I like to call the "do whatever you want" policy. Because of the sexual revolution in the 1960s, our culture has had a distorted view of freedom, which plays out by basically making two rules the catch-all for relationships—first, do whatever you want and whatever feels good, as long as it doesn't hurt anybody else. Second, don't you ever dare to tell anyone whatever they are doing is wrong or could cause hurt, or damage, or not be the best for them.

This means that things that were unheard of before moved to being normal on a grand scale culturally, such as moving in together before you're married and having sex on the first date. (In fact, a recent article on Mashable shows that the average it takes for a relationship to get to that level is ten text messages back and forth, before they've even met. Thanks, Tinder.) In a recent *Vanity Fair* article highlighting the "dating apocalypse" (her words), one girl remarked that it was not uncommon to talk to a guy on Tinder, meet up for sex, and then see him still lying in bed but back on Tinder looking for another girl—while she is getting dressed to leave.

Casual sex.

Porn.

Hooking up.

Living together.

That's the new normal.

And here's where the church made a big mistake (by the way, of course I'm generalizing here, so this doesn't mean every last church or person, but the pervasive ethos of the day). They became reactionary and started defining themselves by what they were against instead of what they were for.

And this is always a bad idea. It can't sustain itself. It doesn't last. It's a short-term solution. The kingdom of God doesn't react to the world; we show the world a better way. There is a difference.

Instead of the church driving the conversation about sexuality, dating, and marriage, we let the culture shape the narrative, and we responded.

Sex is bad.

Don't hold hands.

If you kiss your boyfriend or girlfriend, you're in sin.

Your virginity is your identity.

Ladies, you can't wear spaghetti-strap shirts (because the Lord forbid, it might cause a guy to go into a lustful rage by looking at a woman's shoulder).

So while the "do whatever you want, whenever you want" was one extreme, the church created a second one. One that harbored and cultivated an intensely legalistic subculture, that usually communicated the very opposite of Scripture (in other words, sex and desire are bad and the reason this country is going to hell in a handbasket).

We created a culture that made it more of a point to be a virgin than to be a genuine follower of Jesus who loves Him well, serves the poor, creates justice, and more. We created a culture that cared more about behavior than heart transformation.

A brief scene in the popular show *Shameless* contained some piercing sarcasm highlighting this. There's an episode where the college roommate's girlfriend says she's a virgin. The guy basically questions her and says I thought you and your boyfriend were having sex. To which she responds: "Backdoor only. I'm saving myself for my husband."

To think there isn't some twisted thinking on this subject is an understatement. Being a Christian has become more about being a technical virgin than about actually honoring Him with your body and thoughts and emotions.

I've heard many stories of students at Christian colleges getting married at eighteen or nineteen so they can stop "burning with passion." I'm sure there are tons of people who got married that young for the right reasons, but again, it comes down to motivation. The heart behind the behavior. I know many people who are products of the nineties' evangelicalism who got married more to obey their legalism than because they thought they actually should get married.

I heard someone recently say that we are all refugees of the sexual revolution—the ideas and philosophies put into motion then have left many of us relationally bankrupt. But I'd argue that the same is true for a fundamentalist Christian standpoint. Many of us are refugees and runaways from the purity culture as well.

So we grew up and walked into marriages that exploded with a husband's porn addiction or with an inability to celebrate intimacy because there were so many years of "no, it's bad." And we are left thinking, *What now? Is there a better way? Is there a place somewhere in the middle where boundaries and rules and Scripture is celebrated as God's design for us in our relationships but one that also celebrates a very God-given (not Devil-given) desire in us for intimacy, oneness, a spouse, and relationships?*

And so many in our culture believe this underlying narrative that, to be truly free, there must be no restrictions.

Don't tell me sex should only be in marriage.

Don't tell me what I can and can't do with my body.

And people will ask us sometimes, "Can I have sex before marriage?"

Of course you can. You can do whatever you want. That's just a bad question though.

The better questions are, What will give you the most life? What will give you the most joy? What will give you the most wholeness?

We've bought this lie that personal freedom is the ultimate goal. We have reacted (rightly so, to some degree) against our parents' generation of overbearing legalism and restraint by saying true joy must be found in ultimate, uninhibited freedom.

But it makes me want to ask, what's true freedom?

To me, *true* freedom has restrictions inherently built in. To have *true* freedom, you *have* to have restrictions.

I once heard someone say a fish is truly free in the water. It can flourish and play and eat and live out its full existence—when in the water. But if you take the fish out of the water and put it on land? It dies. Very quickly. The land isn't freedom—the fish wasn't made for it.

Or take the ultimate cliché picture of adventure and freedom in human form—skydiving. At the moment you feel most free, you are actually incredibly restricted. By a suit. By straps. By a backpack with a parachute. Take off those restrictions? You die.

The question isn't, how do I take off all restrictions? The question is, what restrictions are going to lead to the most freedom?

And for sex, that's marriage.

Sex is incredible and life-giving and joyful and intimate and vulnerable and doing exactly what it's supposed to be doing—*in a covenant.*

But when it's with someone who has made no commitment to you for life, it breeds death. Even when it might feel like it's actually ultimate freedom for the moment, just like the skydiver without a chute, sooner or later you will hit the ground. That was my experience, at least.

Because the truth is, if we are letting our bodies say something (I want to be one with you) that our lives aren't willing to (not married, so not fully one), it will backfire and short-circuit.

Sex is too weighty. Too beautiful. Too incredible. To *not* be in marriage.

I like how Tim Keller describes sex, as basically a vow renewal ceremony.[3] Sex becomes this grand picture of your bodies saying what your words did at the altar. In sickness and in health. Until death do us part. I want to be one with you, forever.

Sex in marriage has actually healed parts of me. Where before it brought death, in a beautiful, loving covenant it brought life. When sex is distorted, it can hurt, damage, and confuse. When it's done right, under a promise, in full transparency and vulnerability, it can mend, heal, and soften.

The pure biological fulfillment intertwined with lust in my teenage and college years was simply a distortion. It was like an adult playing in the kiddie pool. Sure, it might cool you off on a hot day, and sure, it might satisfy you, but you were created for *way more*. You were created for the deep side of the pool—better yet, you were created for the ocean—a place of endless exploration, depth, and life. It's not that the kiddie pool is bad. It's that you are painfully missing something if you are in the two-foot water. It doesn't take any work to swim in the kiddie pool. Anyone can do that. But to swim in deep water takes work. Takes practice. Takes discipline. So it is with the boundaries and confines of a marriage. It takes work.

Waking up next to girls whose names I didn't know, in beds I had never slept in before, didn't give me true satisfaction or wholeness. I was never *seen*. I mean, truly seen. The nakedness of the soul and spirit.

But in marriage? I've never felt so vulnerable. I've never felt so seen. So transparent and loved, all at the same time.

TAKEAWAY

We all bring baggage into marriage. But we can also find true and immense healing in marriage. Marriage is the beautiful mystery of two people coming together to create one new entity. Of two people formed day by day into one new creation, one new image of God.

16

JUST THE WAY YOU ARE

(Bruno Mars)

When Jeff and I started dating the second time, we were part of a college ministry in Tacoma, Washington. Jake, Jeff's best friend, had gone to that college and had started a monthly gathering. By the time Jeff and I moved back home, the gathering had grown to about 150 students, with different discipleship groups and a weekly Bible study. On Wednesday nights we would meet at Jeff's and Jake's house, gather in the living room, and learn.

One Valentine's Day I was leading the girls in a study on relationships. I knew that what I had to share wasn't a very popular or well-liked topic to discuss, but the Lord had laid it on my heart, so I had to get it out. I explained to them how our role as women is to be our husbands' helpmates, and that's an extraordinary calling.

As I shared, I could see the wheels spinning for the thirty girls. They looked at me with eyes filled with wonder, as if they had never before heard what I was sharing. They understood what

God meant and could see that His way was really best and for their flourishing and that they had a high calling as women.

We, as women, are called to be helpmates. Genesis 2:18 says, "The LORD God said, 'It is not good for the man to be alone; I will make him a *helper* suitable for him" (NASB). The Hebrew word for "helper" is *ezer*, which means "to help, nourish, sustain, or strengthen."[1] Being an *ezer* takes a lot of strength, wisdom, and honor.

We are called to nurture, support, encourage, cultivate, and to give relief and comfort, which comes naturally to many of us women. It may need to be cultivated in our hearts, but we definitely continue to grow in helping others with joy and selflessness (because it's sometimes really hard!). Now, as believers, we're all called to help and encourage, and as women, we're called to do that with everyone. But in marriage particularly, we're called to be our husbands' support. This role takes courage and strength and incredible sacrifice.

Throughout the Bible, God and the Holy Spirit are both called our Helper. John 14:16 says, "I [Jesus] will ask the Father, and he will give you another Helper, to be with you forever."

The other day I was swinging on our lanai (or porch, as you mainlanders say), choking back tears because the day just felt too heavy for me. It felt a bit impossible. I had so much on my plate and was worried about how the day would go. I had a work deadline fast approaching, and I was stuck. We were trying to sell our house and had multiple showings that week. I was preparing for our trip to the mainland, and on top of everything, our five-month-old wasn't sleeping well. I was tired and weak, and felt like I had no idea what I was doing.

I read Psalm 18 and was reminded of how God is my Helper. I could cry out to him for help, and He would rescue me because he delights in me. He would come to my aid. He would move mountains and send lightning, or whatever it took, to rescue me. I was so comforted by that truth! I felt so alone in my weakness, and yet here God was, telling me that I could run into His arms and find refuge. God was going to walk with me through the day. He'd carry my burdens and help me do the things I needed to get done. He was my support and would sustain me through the day.

I can't say that any of my problems were solved that day. But I had a hope to carry me through the day, a strength that brought joy. A friend texted me to see how I was, and after I shared my burdens with her, she told me she'd bring dinner for our family that night so I didn't have to think about it. My mom brought over flowers to cheer me up, and my best friend texted me a verse and said she was praying for me. I felt so loved, so known and encouraged.

How comforting and beautiful it is that I can be weak because God is strong, and that even more so, He wants me to run to Him and ask Him for help. Second Corinthians 12:9 says, "My grace is sufficient for you, for my power is made perfect in weakness. Therefore I will boast all the more gladly of my weaknesses, so that the power of Christ may rest upon me."

Because God is our Helper, then we know that our role as helper is not inferior, but rather is a role that takes strength and courage. It involves being sensitive to our husbands' needs, listening, praying diligently for them, and being their biggest cheerleaders and their biggest fans. It takes humility to think of them first and put them above ourselves; it takes courage to speak truth and ask the hard questions; it takes faithfulness to continue to pray and nurture when we're exhausted; it takes faith and trust that God is in control and you can go to him yourself and cry out for help.

Women are called to be helpers, but when sin entered the world, God spoke a curse over man, woman, and the serpent. Genesis 3:16 says, "To the woman he said, 'I will surely multiply your pain in childbearing; in pain you shall bring forth children. Your desire shall be contrary to your husband, but he shall rule over you." The curse is twofold; it's wrapped up in childbirth and oppression. We all know that childbirth is extremely painful (and we sing hallelujah for modern medicine!), but what exactly does *oppression* mean here?

Wendy Alsup writes, in *The Gospel-Centered Woman*, that the word *rule* in this verse "is not a term for the kind and grace-filled leadership that Ephesians 5 describes. The term *rule* indicates oppression."[2] That phrase doesn't mean that we, as women, will adore our husbands naturally, but rather it implies a wrongful longing and desire for our husbands, one that is idolatrous. We'll desire men above God and seek to find our fulfillment in them, more than in, or other than in God. We'll seek their approval, base our identity and worth on what they say or don't say, what they do or don't do.

One of my biggest struggles is my desire to be in control. I want to be in charge, to call the shots, to know what's happening and what's going to happen, to control my circumstances. It's become so common that I don't even realize it half the time. Lately I've been getting anxious about my baby's sleep. I worry that he'll wake up too early or not sleep enough or that he'll be unhappy. I get anxious about his schedule and "what if" something doesn't go as planned. Although I'm working hard to make sure he has all he needs, a lot of those things are out of my control. And it's so hard to give it over to the Lord constantly. We doubt that God's in control, or we believe the lie that He isn't at work or doesn't have the power to do what (we think) is best.

When Eve was in the garden of Eden, she felt like God was holding out on her, so she took the reins of her life and did it her way. God had told Adam that they could eat of any tree in the garden, except the tree of the knowledge of good and evil. God knew that if they ate of this tree, then they would stop relying on Him because they wouldn't need Him. He wanted intimacy with them, to be in constant fellowship with His children, but if they ate of this tree, fellowship would be broken. Adam and Eve would rely on themselves instead of on God.

Then, when Satan came to entice Eve, he twisted God's word and made her doubt Him, and she fell into the trap. Genesis 3:6 says, "When the woman saw that the tree was good for food, and that it was a delight to the eyes, and that the tree was to be desired to make one wise, she took of its fruit and ate, and she also gave some to her husband who was with her, and he ate."

While it's easy to blame Eve, when you really read that verse, it sounds like she was logical and thought it through. It was good to eat, it was beautiful, it could make you wise. But God told her not to eat it. Instead of trusting His word, she went ahead and did what she thought was best. She didn't believe He was for her good, and so she took control. Then when God came looking for them and asked what happened, Eve blamed the serpent. She twisted the truth. Yes, the serpent had deceived her, but she was the one to act; she was the one who ate the fruit. She had a choice: to believe God or believe Satan. And she took the latter.

We're not so different from Eve. How often are we tempted to take control of a matter, to not believe God's Word or that He's all powerful or for us? How often do we think we know what's best, for ourselves, our husbands, our friends, our children?

My eating disorder all started because I wanted guys to notice me. I wanted their attention and approval so badly, I went to great lengths to change who I was so they'd notice me. I tried to control my life, whatever hard circumstance was going on at the time, through controlling what I ate and didn't eat.

Often the desire to control is played out in manipulation. Some women try to control by manipulating the guys in their lives. This manipulation is usually coming out of a place of insecurity. I have a good friend who dated a girl and was head over heels for her. He wanted to marry her and was starting to make plans in that direction. They talked about marriage a lot. But then, she broke up with him, and my friend was heartbroken.

Instead of cutting ties and going their separate ways, however, they continued talking. For years. My friend knew it wasn't for the best, but he had high hopes that one day they'd get back together. He would go through phases of unfriending her on Facebook, unfollowing her on Instagram, deleting her phone number from his phone. But she'd keep coming back. She'd call and text. They'd run into each other. She would flirt and know the exact thing to say to keep him around.

She wanted to call the shots as to when they could talk and not talk. She manipulated him when they dated by talking about marriage way too prematurely in order to experience some type of intimacy, and she manipulated him long after. She kept him around just in case her feelings changed or in case she wanted to have a guy to talk to when she was lonely or needed a friend. She didn't consider his feelings, however, and gave him false hope. Manipulating someone else is selfish. If you know you're not going to get back together, then you have to cut ties, and let go. Let the other person be free to heal so they can be available for the person God does have for them.

When you are in a healthy relationship, you don't have to manipulate, because you're each seeking the good of the other. You're both honest and patient. The beautiful thing about marriage is, you're both surrendering your control and giving yourself to each other, and in that vulnerability, there's great joy and security.

Manipulation and control can slip into marriage too. It tries to creep into my heart in my marriage with Jeff.

I remember when Kinsley was about one and a half, and Jeff and I were in the trenches of disciplining. I mean, you're always training your child, and disciplining a lot during the younger years, but during this age we were trying to figure out how to discipline her. We were trying to work together to come up with a philosophy for our family and what worked best for Kinsley. I was pregnant with our son, Kannon, at the time, too, so needless to say, I was a bit more tired and irritable.

And I was really struggling with my desire to control. Jeff was being an incredible dad, wanting to be so involved and lead our family. But I was resisting. I wanted to call the shots. I wanted to decide on what disciplining method to use and have him just follow along. Because I was the mom.

WHEN YOU ARE IN A HEALTHY RELATIONSHIP, YOU DON'T HAVE TO MANIPULATE, BECAUSE YOU'RE EACH SEEKING THE GOOD OF THE OTHER.

One Wednesday morning I had my mom friends over for a Bible study, and the one leading that day, who was a bit older than us and had kids in high school, shared how she loves submitting to her husband. I laughed and made a remark under my breath: "Man, if only I could say the same thing." And it hit me—how I wanted to take the reins, push Jeff aside, and assert myself as though I knew what was best.

The Holy Spirit spoke to my heart that morning and showed me how I was in the wrong. I realized that I can rejoice in submitting to Jeff, too, because God has blessed me with an incredible husband who loves Jesus and wants to lead our home. He wants to have a vision for our family, to be present, to lead us with grace and truth.

God doesn't want Jeff to forcefully lead our family, to treat me like my opinion doesn't exist; nor does He intend for me to argue with Jeff or demean him every time I disagree with him on a topic. He wants us to listen to each other, to work things out together. He wants me to trust Jeff because I can trust that He is working in him, and He wants Jeff to be sensitive to my intuitions and gracefully lead our home.

Jeff and I are a team. He doesn't just make plans and not include me, or expect me to automatically follow his every idea and thought. Rather, we run everything by each other, and if we're on the same page, then it's a go. God put us together, including our strengths, so we work together. But I realized that I could trust God to work in Jeff and help him make the best decisions for our family, and I could enjoy working together with Jeff instead of trying to push him aside. When we work in this rhythm, it's the best. It's how God intended it.

TAKEAWAY

Wives have an extraordinary calling as helpmates, a role that takes courage, strength, and sacrifice. God wants us to run to Him when our role becomes overwhelming. We can trust God to work in our husbands so that we can become healthy teams, each seeking the good of the other, reflecting His beautiful plan for marriage.

17

UNPACK YOUR HEART

(Phillip Phillips)

Alyssa and I love coffee.

And when I say we love coffee, I mean we are obsessed with coffee, and I, especially, nerd out on all the different ways to make it at home (depending on the day, I'll rotate between Chemex, French press, and AeroPress). Coffee (and good books) are my love language. I actually have a T-shirt that says, "I love you more than coffee, but don't make me prove it."

But I also have some rules when it comes to drinking coffee.

It has to be in a certain mug.

I have to drink it all in one sitting, or I throw it out.

And I take it black. I don't mess around with that poison folks call "creamer."

Alyssa, however, is a little different. She likes hers with a little bit of creamer. She nurses it all day, which means she usually microwaves it a couple of times throughout the day—which makes me shudder. And she'll leave it places—in the car, in the bedroom, or outside on our porch.

A couple of weeks ago I was in the car and started to smell something a little sour. Sadly, because we have two kids under three and our car is basically a war zone, this is not uncommon. But I decided I'd find the culprit.

I looked down to my left in the cupholder at the bottom of the door and saw a travel coffee mug. Seeing as it was a little out of sight and could easily stay there without being noticed, I knew that was the culprit.

But instead of just throwing it away (mug included, because it was that bad) or dumping it out right away, I decided to look inside. That's when I almost died.

Seriously, the Lord almost took me home after that stench. I'll spare you the details, but let's just say the creamer and coffee, sitting there over multiple days, in the hot Maui sun, didn't end well.

And it got me thinking: What a terrible yet truthful picture of how a lot of us deal with our past, our baggage, and things done before our marriage. Whether we like it or not, we bring *everything* into marriage. Our experiences, our hurts, our failures, our past, our shame, our guilt, and our brokenness.

Yet so many of us don't face it head-on but instead try to pretend it doesn't exist or won't affect us. And like the coffee, it stays close to us, out of sight, out of mind.

Until our baggage starts to smell. And then it gets worse. And worse. And worse.

Our past—our baggage, and everything we bring into the marriage—is a ticking time bomb that usually goes off sooner or later. And it prevents us not only from true intimacy but also from true joy.

God has so much more for us and our marriages.

There are two ways we bring things into our relationships: by things we have done and by things that have been done to us.

Sadly, in our culture, things like rape, abuse, and emotional trauma are commonplace. I've gotten e-mails from countless folks detailing a horrid experience when they were younger and how it's crippling their marriage—preventing intimacy, creating division, and simply placing a huge wall between spouses. These aren't things we've done, but things that have been done against us.

In one of the more fascinating and heartbreaking books I've read in years, Dr. Bessel van der Kolk details how trauma can literally affect our physiology, brain chemistry, and other parts of our humanness. The title of the book itself is chilling and telling—*The Body Keeps the Score*.

One in five Americans have been molested.

One in four grew up with alcoholics.

One in three couples have engaged in physical violence.[1]

Even if we try to forget the trauma, even if we try to move on, unless we've actually *dealt* with it and found healing, our body doesn't. Our body doesn't forget. Unless we deal with it, "trauma literally reshapes both body and brain, compromising sufferers' capacities for pleasure, engagement, self-control, and trust."

One of Dr. Van der Kolk's most crucial findings was that, without proper help, care, and healing, your life and growth essentially stop. You lose your ability to integrate new experiences into your life, and this is incredibly detrimental in the most intimate relationship possible—a marriage. He tells a story of a support group he led, with PTSD victims from World War II. In many ways they welcomed him into the brotherhood and even honored him at Christmastime with a World War II–era watch. Yet, as he recalls, it was "a sad memento of the year their lives had effectively stopped: 1944."

Trauma creates a loop in our systems; we can no longer move forward, but instead we organize our entire lives around the past trauma as if it were still happening. Everything is seen through the lens of the past. But the most striking is that this is physiological. You actually start to experience life through a different nervous system—one where your energy is mostly focused on "suppressing chaos, at the expense of spontaneous involvement in their life." Basically, you use all your energy just to stay sane and calm and collected, and you have no energy left to live a flourishing life.

But my favorite part of Van der Kolk's research is a little section on the detriment and dark side of pharmacology, and how our culture sees pills and prescriptions as the answer—which, by the way, he admits, is so needed and great, but he asks the question, have we swung too far?

One sentence from the end of the chapter has stuck with me. Dr. Van der Kolk says that the "brain disease model" (aka seeing drugs as the primary answer) overlooks the truth that "our capacity to destroy one another is matched by our capacity to heal one another. Restoring relationships and community is central to restoring well-being."[2]

The very same thing that can destroy us—human relationships—also has the power to heal us.

I think of the wife who was abused as a child and physical touch practically makes her scream, until the husband over and over again, over the course of years, continues to apply a healing touch—one of tenderness, gentleness, and grace. Restoring the beauty and power of touch to her and in their relationship.

I think of the husband who is an alcoholic because his dad abandoned him as a child and that's his way of coping, yet who has a wife who helps him find freedom because of her everyday reassurance that she is there for the long haul and isn't going anywhere, modeling the picture of Jesus, who tells us He will never leave us or forsake us.

Because of the intimacy provided in a marriage, one spouse has such a powerful opportunity to be a healing agent in the other spouse's story. Sometimes it takes years, and it's hard to persevere day after hard day, but the covenant of faithfulness to each other—slowly but surely—creates a bond and healing that lasts forever.

THE VERY SAME
THING THAT
CAN DESTROY
US—HUMAN
RELATIONSHIPS—
ALSO HAS
THE POWER
TO HEAL US.

•

On the flip side of sins that have been done against us, there are ones that have been done by us.

This is more true to my story.

I came into my relationship with Alyssa with so much baggage, shame, and hurt. I realized I had crossed lines I never should've crossed in past relationships and done things I never should have done. I had images and thoughts and flashbacks that brought a weight and burden into our relationship.

And it was only exacerbated by the fact that Alyssa hadn't even held a guy's hand until we started dating in our early twenties.

But there have been a couple of things that have brought us to a place of wholeness.

The first is, I apologized. A lot.

I knew I had given myself to others in many distorted ways before Alyssa and I met. That was a sin against Alyssa and our covenant (and a sin against those other girls and their future husbands). And I had to repent.

I remember writing a couple of Facebook messages to past girlfriends (not awkward at all, right?) and apologizing for how I treated them. For how I dishonored them. For how I disrespected them. And I asked for their forgiveness.

I don't know if that's for everyone, but I do know I felt a nag and burden until I did. And when you're a follower of Jesus, apologizing and asking for forgiveness is your job, and God can handle and be in charge of the rest. I'm not sure whether those messages maybe created a little thought in those women's minds about Jesus and His grace, or whether the women were disgusted and upset I messaged them at all. But I'll leave that up to God.

I then realized I needed to tell Alyssa. Early on in our relationship, we were sitting in the car after a date, and I told her everything. I remember being terrified. Here was this varsity perfect holy Pleasantville Christian—and then me.

But I'll never forget that night. She didn't flinch. She didn't even look hurt (even though she may have been!). Her eyes and demeanor were piercing. She just said, "I forgive you. That's how Jesus sees you now. Jeff, you're clean."

In that car, something clicked. It was such a beautiful moment for me to realize she was right. That *is* how Jesus sees me.

And that's how He sees you.

We are spotless.

Clean.

Righteous.

Made new.

Resurrected.

Washed.

Not because of *who we are* but because of *what He's done.*

The best part about that is, since it's based on what He's done, our standing can never change. Because it's done. It's finished. Our sin is gone. He took all our shame and guilt and pain and past and absorbed it into Himself up on the Cross. And then when He died, it did too. He put it in the grave. And on that magnificent day we call Easter, He walked out of the grave. And left our sin in the tomb. In the home of death, where it belongs. And new life is now ours. Freely given.

Debt canceled.

So the fight isn't about trying to get free or to get our sins forgiven or to be made new. The fight is about *believing those things are already true.*

And looking shame and evil and Satan right in the face, and saying *no.* That's not true. My debt has been cancelled. Nice try.

It reminds me of the underbelly of debt collection agencies. You know, those people who call you and pretty much harass you to pay debt you almost certainly don't remember? (My only experience with them was when I was nineteen and an unnoticed overdraft fee put me like seven dollars in debt, which turned into like one hundred dollars of debt because of all the crazy fees and interest charges. I think I overdrafted because I was trying to get some Peach-O Rings and an Arnold Palmer from 7-Eleven. The most expensive Peach-O Rings I ever bought.)

But a lot of people don't realize just how crazy the debt collection world really is. Essentially what happens is, debt is repackaged and resold over and over and over again. The bank will sell it to a collection agency for maybe seventy cents on the dollar (so if the whole debt is worth $100 million, they'll sell it for $70 million), and then that collection agency tries to hound the people to pay their debt so they can make more money than they invested.

And once they tap out the debt file, guess what they do?

Sell it down the line to a little more sketchy agency. And this happens over and over again, to the point where there is usually one last stop on this terrible hierarchy of debt collections. A debt file will end up getting sold for literally a penny on the dollar to a law firm. And these lawyers will then sue you for your debt. They'll call you and give you a court date.

In Jake Halpern's brilliant book, *Bad Paper*, he followed a few folks to the court to see what actually happened. Right outside of the courtroom, the lawyer would corner the person being sued and say, "Let's just settle. Your debt is $5,000 but give us $3,000 and we can call it all off and not go into this courtroom." Almost always they pay. Because of the intimidation and because they probably do owe that money (not always, since there are lots of mistakes in the selling of others' debt).

But in Halpern's book, he saw something pretty crazy happen. They step into the courtroom, and the intimidation continues. The lawyer tries a couple of things that don't work, so the lawyer steps outside to talk to whoever is really running the show, and comes back in and says they are dropping the case. The debt is gone.

Halpern was incredibly confused. All that intimidation and work for nothing?

So later he asked a lawyer who specializes in representing low-income debtors. And the lawyer said he wasn't surprised at all that the case was dismissed, because "all a debtor had to do was show up and utter the 'magic words.'"[3]

"What are the magic words?" Halpern asked.

"Prove your case," replied the lawyer.

He then went on to say that usually the debt has been bought and sold so many times, that by the time the lawyers who sue for it get it, there is almost zero record of the debt. No proof. There is virtually no possible way the proper records could have made it down the line intact. It's like a big corporate game of telephone (mind you, with the selling party having zero incentive to keep accurate records, because they just sold the debt and washed their hands of it). By then it's usually just a Microsoft Excel file with a name, a phone number, possibly an address, and the outstanding debt amount. No way to corroborate it, no original contracts, no show of interest or principal.

And so when it gets to court, they have no case, no ability to prove the debt. The lawyers hope it never gets there. And, probably 99 percent of the time, it never does because of all the endless calls, and intimidation and legal speak and settlements.

I remember reading that story and instantly thinking of Satan and his tactics against us, especially in relationships. (Now, of course, I'm not saying we should go into financial debt, because we shouldn't. Alyssa and I believe that debt can be an incredible strain on marriage—shoutout to Dave Ramsey!)

But Satan will do the very same thing. He'll intimidate. Bring up past thoughts and pictures. Remind you of how guilty you are. Of all the shame. The hurt. The pain.

And I've been there. And felt that. And still do.

But it's in those moments that we say the same thing. *Prove your case.*

And he can't.

Because Jesus canceled "the record of debt that stood against us with its legal demands. This he set aside, nailing it to the cross. He disarmed the rulers and authorities and put them to open shame, by triumphing over them in him" (Colossians 2:14–15).[4]

And so the minute Satan tries to creep into your marriage and heap shame and guilt and your past sins on you, you don't need to defend yourself. Just point to the cross. That's where victory was won. That's where your debt was cancelled. In a tomb two thousand years ago right outside Jerusalem. It's been buried and can never be thrown back in your face again.

So remember that baggage you bring into marriage the minute you say "I do" at the altar? Don't run from it. Don't hide it in an emotional closet, in hopes that it'll go away. It won't. It'll start to stink and only get worse.

Stare it right in the face, and know that under Jesus your debt is gone. And healing is possible. And you're not alone.

•

We must also consider not only the things we bring into the marriage, or the things done against us, but also the things we continually do in the marriage.

It's in those moments, especially early on in the marriage, when you realize that the first year of marriage is very much a crucible. When two lives are completely thrown together in all areas (finances, creativity, career, sexuality, and more), there is bound to be friction. And in that friction, we are tempted to think the other person is the problem. I'd be lying if I said this didn't happen with Alyssa and me.

Why doesn't she just act more like me?

Why doesn't she do it this way?

It all comes down to framework: If you believe marriage is to make you happy, then you will be severely disappointed. (Now, does marriage make you happy? It sure does for us! But that's not the point of marriage.) And when you believe that, you argue and fight differently. If your personal happiness is paramount, then anything that impedes that, like all your spouse's differences, you'll push back against.

What if marriage isn't meant to make you happy but to make you holy?

And I don't mean holy in the simplistic (actually false) definition of strict morality and whether you do this or don't do that.

Holiness by definition simply means set apart, or sacred, or my favorite—different.

And, so in some ways, you can say that marriage is about making you different.

Or another way to put it is, marriage is about making you look more like Jesus.

When you realize that you no longer see disagreements or differences or your spouse's peculiarities as annoying or maddening but instead see them as opportunities to grow into your true self, then the image of God is reflected to be more and more like Jesus.

It's like sandpaper—if you have two pieces of sandpaper and you rub them against each other, there will be enormous friction and resistance. But the longer you do that, the more they begin to smooth each other out.

That's kind of what marriage does. It's the smoothing, or the making, of one *new* image in both of you.

Alyssa isn't the roadblock to my personal happiness. She's actually God's gift to me, to make me a more full image of Jesus.

And to find my true self, I don't need to leave the marriage when it gets hard. I need to embrace the friction. The biggest lie we sometimes believe in our culture is we need to leave our marriage to find our true selves.

Or another way I see it framed in movies and conversations with others is as a constant battle to pick between a spouse, and kids, or finding yourself. I know marriages end for all types of reasons. And I know, sadly, that some do need to end. Abuse. Adultery. Gaslighting.

WHAT IF
MARRIAGE
ISN'T MEANT
TO MAKE
YOU HAPPY
BUT TO
MAKE YOU
HOLY?

But I also know a lot of marriages that ended simply because of lies—lies one or both of the partners believed. That if they wanted to be truly happy, their marriage should end. Not realizing that the breaking point of *self* is usually the exact moment a deep and lasting marriage takes root.

But maybe instead of thinking we need to leave a marriage, we need to expand our definition of marriage so it's not so rigid, cold, and narrow that only one spouse "wins" and the other needs to take the backseat. A true marriage, and one that brings the most joy when lived in, is one that celebrates and grows each person simultaneously.

Because a marriage that is big enough for both people to flourish and use their gifting and be creative is what will produce the best results anyway. Marriage is the tough work of two individuals with their own dreams, goals, and talents coming together and almost restarting in a way—building up new dreams and goals as a couple. And it takes work. And it's messy. And there will be different seasons. But don't give up until you get there.

NOW WHAT?

A forty-year marriage—what all of us are shooting for. To grow old together, to be so close that you finish each other's sentences. A look between the two of you holds more communication and weight than one thousand words shared by a younger couple.

But imagine getting near the finish line, and forgetting it all. Every last memory and date and up and down. That one time you fell into the pool at your aunt's Fourth of July party and we laughed until we cried. That time we prayed on the hospital floor for God to save the baby, and He did. Or that time He didn't seem to. Or that fateful day we met; we recounted the story probably one thousand times over the years.

Imagine it all disappearing. Not a trace.

That's what happened with Robertson McQuilkin and his wife, Muriel. He remembers the first time she repeated a story to the couple they met on vacation, just five minutes after telling them the story the first time. He thought it strange but funny. Looking back, that was the moment he realized his wife started to fade.

With a severe case of Alzheimer's, she continually worsened—to the point where she could barely speak in full sentences, and even then there was confusion.

In many ways, the woman he had married forty years before didn't exist anymore.

But he disagreed. He promised to love her unto death, and the wife he made that promise to was still living and breathing.

So what did he do? He quit his job as the president of a prominent seminary and retired much earlier than planned (which probably meant a much lower retirement package).

In a beautiful letter he wrote more than a decade ago upon his retirement, he notes:

> She is such a delight to me. I don't have to care for her, I get to. One blessing is the way she is teaching me so much—about love, for example, God's love.
>
> Muriel cannot speak in sentences now, only in phrases and words, and often words that make little sense: "no" when she means "yes," for example. But she can say one sentence, and she says it often: "I love you."
>
> She not only says it, she acts it. The board arranged for a companion to stay in our home so I could go daily to the office. During those two years it became increasingly difficult to keep Muriel home. As soon as I left, she would take out after me. With me, she was content; without me, she was distressed, sometimes terror stricken. The walk to school is a mile round trip. She would make that trip as many as ten times a day. Sometimes at night, when I helped her undress, I found bloody

feet. When I told our family doctor, he choked up. "Such love," he said simply. Then, after a moment, "I have a theory that the characteristics developed across the years come out at times like these." I wish I loved God like that—desperate to be near him at all times. Thus she teaches me, day by day.

I came across the common contemporary wisdom in this morning's newspaper in a letter to a national columnist: "I ended the relationship because it wasn't meeting my needs," the writer explained. The counselor's response was predictable: "What were your needs that didn't get met by him in the relationship? Do you still have these same needs? What would he have to do to fill these needs? Could he do it?" Needs for communication, understanding, affirmation, common interests, sexual fulfillment—the list goes on. If the needs are not met, split. He offered no alternatives. I once reflected on the eerie irrelevance of every one of those criteria for me.[1]

McQuilkin's story has stuck with me for years, since I first heard it. I can think of no better example of what the real covenantal love of marriage looks like than this.

And this is what we hope this whole book is about—digging, showing, asking—what is the love we were made for? In McQuilkin's story we see a glimpse, knowing that he himself points to Jesus' love for us as the motivation that enables him to live similarly.

Alyssa and I know that a huge variety of folks are going to read this book: people in a good marriage, people in an unhealthy marriage, people dating and not sure if they want to break up, people dating who are about to get engaged, single folks who desire a relationship, and single folks who are in a season of contentment but want to learn more.

We truly hope this book and our story encouraged you in some way. Maybe made you ask different questions, changed your outlook on relationships, or brought healing in places where it was desperately needed.

ACKNOWLEDGMENTS

To our community: To our parents, married friends, single friends, older friends, and younger friends, our marriage is what it is because of you. Thank you for pouring into us and allowing us to walk this life with you. Looking at your lives and relationships, we are so proud of each of you and thankful that God gave us such incredible people to follow and learn from.

To Curtis, Mike, Sealy, and Matt: Thanks for believing in us. There would be no book without you. You guys feel like family, and we're so thankful to have you guys be our sounding board, defenders, counselors, and coaches.

To Brian, Jeff, Jenny, Janene, Karen, Jessica, Webb, Kathie, Aryn, Stephanie, and Tiffany: We have both dreamed of being authors. Thanks for taking a chance on us. You guys are the most top-notch team and it's an honor to work with such great people. We are forever indebted to you all.

To Mallory: You rocked the interior page design!

ACKNOWLEDGMENTS

To Ashton: Thanks for always using your incredible creativity to make some of the best book covers we've ever seen. This book wouldn't be the same without you.

To Angela: Your ability to think how we think and understand what we are *trying* to say and help us say it better is a true gift. Thank you. You are crazy gifted, and this book would not be what it is without you.

NOTES

Chapter 1: Where Is the Love?

1. http://www.theatlantic.com/health/archive/2014/03/on-late-in
   -life-virginity-loss/284412/.
2. Katie Hafner, "Researchers Confront an Epidemic of Loneliness,"
   The New York Times, September 5, 2016, https://www.nytimes
   .com/2016/09/06/health/lonliness-aging-health-effects.html.
3. Shmuley Boteach and Pamela Anderson, "Take the Pledge:
   No More Indulging Porn," *The Wall Street Journal,* August 31,
   2016, http://www.wsj.com/articles/take-the-pledge-no-more
   -indulging-porn-1472684658.
4. Justin Karter, "Percentage of Americans on Antidepressants
   Nearly Doubles," Mad in America, November 6, 2015, https://
   www.madinamerica.com/2015/11/percentage-of-americans
   -on-antidepressants-nearly-doubles/.
5. Alex Leff, "'Til 2013 do us part? Mexico mulls 2-year marriage,"
   Reuters, September 29, 2011, http://www.reuters.com/article
   /us-mexico-marriage-idUSTRE78S6TX20110929.
6. "Sex Dolls That Talk Back," *The New York Times,* June 11, 2015,
   http://www.nytimes.com/2015/06/12/technology/robotica
   -sexrobot-realdoll.html.

7. "The Most Common Word in Porn Sites Comments Is . . . ," Fight the New Drug, January 21, 2015, http://fightthenewdrug .org/oh-the-irony-this-is-the-most-used-word-in-porn-comments/.
8. Christopher West, *Theology of the Body for Beginners* (Milwaukee, WI: Ascension Press, 2004).
9. Wendell Berry, *Sex Economy, Freedom, & Community* (New York: Pantheon Books, 1993), 138–139.

Chapter 3
1. "Stats," Fatherhood Factor, accessed May 3, 2017, http://father hoodfactor.com/us-fatherless-statistics/.

Chapter 4: Riding Solo
1. Job 42:2.
2. Psalm 23:6.
3. Ephesians 3:20.
4. Lamentations 3:25, Psalm 37:7, and Romans 10:11.

Chapter 8: Bleeding Love
1. 1 Corinthians 13:7.

Chapter 9: We Are Never Ever Getting Back Together
1. Kirsten King, "I Don't Owe Anyone My Body," Buzzfeed, January 27, 2016, https://www.buzzfeed.com/kirstenking/i-dont-owe -anyone-my-body?utm_term=.mdlye2q20#.ec6GERdR9.

Chapter 13: All of Me
1. Deuteronomy 24:5.

Chapter 14: Let's Get It On
1. Ed Wheat, MD and Gaye Wheat, *Intended for Pleasure* (Ada, MI: Revell, 2010).

2. Sharon Jaynes, *Praying for Your Husband from Head to Toe* (Sisters, OR: Multnomah, 2013).

3. Rebekah Lyons, "Be, Still, and Know – Free Study," http://rebekahlyons.com/updates/be-still-and-know-free-study.

Chapter 15: Let's Talk About Sex

1. Jenell Williams Paris, *The End of Sexual Identity* (Westmont, IL: InterVarsity, 2011), 12.

2. Ronald Rolheiser, *The Holy Longing* (New York: Image Catholic Books, 2009), 196.

3. Tim Keller, "The Gospel and Sex," Q, accessed May 3, 2017, http://208.106.253.109/essays/the-gospel-and-sex.aspx?page=1.

Chapter 16: Just the Way You Are

1. Wendy Horgur Alsup, *The Gospel Centered Woman* (CreateSpace Independent Publishing Platform, 2013), 12.

2. Ibid., 20.

Chapter 17: Unpack Your Heart

1. Body Keeps Score.

2. Ibid., 38.

3. Bad Paper, 189.

4. Colossians 2:14–15.

Now What?

1. Robertson McQuilkin, "Living by Vows," *Christianity Today*, February 2, 2004, accessed July 11, 2017, http://www.christianitytoday.com/ct/2004/februaryweb-only/2-9-11.0.html?start=3.

ADDITIONAL RESOURCES

The Body Keeps the Score by Bessel van der Kolk

Counterfeit Gods by Timothy Keller

The End of Sex by Donna Freitas

The End of Sexual Identity by Jenell Williams Paris

From Eternity to Here by Frank Viola

The Holy Longing by Ronald Rolheiser

Loveology by John Mark Comer

The Meaning of Marriage by Timothy Keller

The Moral Vision of The New Testament by Richard B. Hays

Not Just Good, but Beautiful, Helen Alvaré (editor)

Surprised by Hope by N. T. Wright

Theology of the Body for Beginners by Christopher West

ABOUT THE AUTHORS

Jeff and Alyssa Bethke live in Maui with their three-year-old daughter, Kinsley, and one-year-old son, Kannon. They are the authors of the books *Jesus > Religion*, *It's Not What You Think*, and *Spoken For*. In addition to writing, they make YouTube videos and host a podcast that can be found on iTunes. They also have a yellow lab named Aslan and enjoy reading good books and drinking good coffee during their downtime.

**FINISHED THE BOOK
AND LOOKING FOR
A WAY TO BUILD A LOVE
THAT LASTS?**

———

*That's why Alyssa and I created
the Love That Lasts Experience*

─── IT INCLUDES ───

01

LOVE THAT LASTS FOR MEN AND
LOVE THAT LASTS FOR WOMEN
GUIDEBOOKS.

02

12 VIDEO LESSONS BY OUR MARRIAGE
MENTORS ON 12 BIG TOPICS.

03

THE DEEP LOVE ASSESSMENT-A FUN
10 PAGE CUSTOM REPORT ON YOUR
RELATIONSHIP AND AN EASY WAY TO
GET CLOSER TO EACH OTHER.

04

A PRIVATE FACEBOOK GROUP TO
JOIN WITH ALYSSA AND ME.

GO TO ˅

LOVETHATLASTS.CO/UPGRADE

AND GET THE COMPLETE
EXPERIENCE FOR ONLY

───

$79 DOLLARS
(NORMALY $144)